PLEASE STAY TO
THE ADJOURNMENT

PLEASE STAY TO THE ADJOURNMENT

John Taylor, M.P.

*to David
with best wishes*

John

December 2003

BREWIN BOOKS

First published by
Brewin Books Ltd, 56 Alcester Road,
Studley, Warwickshire B80 7LG in 2003
www.brewinbooks.com

© John Taylor 2003

All rights reserved.

ISBN 1 85858 244 X

The moral right of the author has been asserted.

A Cataloguing in Publication Record
for this title is available from the British Library.

Typeset in Caslon
Printed in Great Britain by
Warwick Printing Company Limited.

Contents

Foreword	*Author's Note*	vi
Prelude	*An Episode In The Whips Office*	vii
Chapter 1	*Air Raid Shelters - Part 1*	1
Chapter 2	*Air Raid Shelters - Part 2*	4
Chapter 3	*Lancashire*	5
Chapter 4	*Eversfield School*	7
Chapter 5	*An Interlude On Ancient Monuments*	11
Chapter 6	*Bromsgrove School*	14
Chapter 7	*A Set Back (1960 - 1961)*	20
Chapter 8	*Aspirations*	22
Chapter 9	*An Interlude On Golf*	24
Chapter 10	*Practising The Law*	28
Chapter 11	*Beginnings Of Politics*	39
Chapter 12	*Councillor*	42
Chapter 13	*The West Midlands County Council - Part 1*	44
Chapter 14	*An Interlude On Dudley East*	47
Chapter 15	*The West Midlands County Council - Part 2*	52
Chapter 16	*The European Parliament - Part 1*	59
Chapter 17	*The European Parliament - Part 2*	63
Chapter 18	*The European Parliament - Part 3*	68
Chapter 19	*An Interlude On Cricket*	69
Chapter 20	*Member Of Parliament*	73
Chapter 21	*Back Benchers And Committees*	75
Chapter 22	*The Whips Office*	82
Chapter 23	*The Lord Chancellor's Department*	89
Chapter 24	*The Department Of Trade And Industry*	96
Chapter 25	*An Interlude On Islands*	101
Chapter 26	*The Night Of 1997*	106
Chapter 27	*A New Start*	109
Chapter 28	*A Whip Again*	113
Chapter 29	*Northern Ireland*	118
Chapter 30	*Secretaries*	122
Chapter 31	*My Father*	123
Index		127

Foreword

Author's Note

At my age I know who I am.

I am the first to realise that I am not a very consequential person. Indeed I regret that I could not have been the originator of the title "Diary of a Nobody".

My beloved Conservative Party at various different times initially refused me access to the approved list of Local Government candidates, the approved list of European Parliamentary candidates and the approved list of Westminster Parliamentary candidates.

Despite this, I went on to become the leader of the second largest local authority in England, the Deputy Leader of the Conservative Group in the European Parliament and the first ever junior minister to the Lord Chancellor, representing him in the House of Commons.

At school, as a fourteen year old, I was preached against by the Chaplain for remarks made by me in the Debating Society.

Much more importantly, I have holed in one at golf and taken four wickets in four balls at cricket (all bowled).

These are the happy reflections of an observant, exuberant, eclectically interested, but timid man. The paradox is that I could never resist a challenge and "jumped out of my socks" to achieve whatever I achieved.

There is an interest to declare. There usually is. I am a man of privilege. That is to say I was loved as a child and given a good education. There are no other privileges.

Prelude

An Episode In The Whips Office

Whipping In Government - Rebellion - Government Defeat?

We had an enormous rebellion on our hands. We were considering Lords Amendments to the Health and Medicine Bill. It was 1st November 1988. Not for the first time in British post-war history the issue was NHS charges for spectacles and dentures. There were two critical votes looming, one on each.

As ever, the truly professional requirement of a well-run Government Whips Office was to have a better measurement of the scale of the rebellion than the rebels had themselves. We did. This one was really serious.

We were working against a general and time-honoured difficulty which is that if a rebellion succeeds, the rebels are perceived as heroes, which is inconvenient, or, thought to have been right, which is much worse.

A good Whip knows that rebels are not heroes and that they are wrong and that they must be defeated. Winners write history.

We also had a more poignant, particular difficulty which became clearer as the vote approached. On the day immediately following the fateful divisions, Margaret Thatcher was to fly to Poland to meet General Jaruzelski on a heads-of-government visit. Poland was still under a rigid regime but in spite of that, or maybe because of that, Poland greatly admired the 'Iron Lady' of western democracy.

For Margaret Thatcher to have arrived in Warsaw with two defeats in her own Parliament merely hours before would have been bitter and demeaning for her and incomprehensible to her Polish hosts.

We followed all the usual procedures exhaustively. In as much as some of the rebels might need to be tackled and confronted directly, that would be done. But not all would be treated that way. Many of the rebels were the subject of much more careful persuasion, consideration and handling. Not infrequently the collective search of the Whips Office was for the identity of the person, almost certainly not a member of the Office themselves, to whom a particular rebel might listen or by whom he or she might be persuaded.

We went through the list of the names of the parliamentary party endlessly. Individual members of the office reported back on their efforts to reduce the rebellion by reference to that part of the list of names for which they were personally responsible. A potential abstainer here or there who might be persuaded to vote for us after all; a vote against that might be persuaded into an abstention. Seldom could conversions be expected any more than that. The office met again and again.

At one stage, towards the end, the meeting fell silent. No one seemed to have anything more useful to say. Apart from the Thatcher factor, we were looking at a possible two billion-pound rupture of the government's budget and one or two possible cabinet resignations.

Tristan[1] broke the silence and the tension. "Thank God it's only a game". We laughed as a kind of release. We knew it wasn't a game.

The fact was that on the numbers we had before us the outcome was, as they say, too close to call. We had by far the best intelligence in Parliament and, even with that, it was a vote or two either way.

But Tristan had broken the tension for a moment long enough for the Chief Whip to provide a final, critical instruction to his office. He told us all, and included himself, that we should get up and walk out of the Office together directly into Members' Lobby with our chins up and smiling. The dispersal of our meeting would be observed, the grapevine would be alerted. The Chief's instinct was right. There would be some rebels who needed only a hint that the whips were on top of the situation to desert the disaster of being part of a *losing* rebellion.

The evening wore on tensely through a series of immaterial divisions until the first critical vote came at 10.07pm. Notwithstanding a theoretical majority of almost a hundred, we won by sixteen. But sixteen was enough. The second critical vote came at 1.03am and we won by eight. Even eight was enough. Even though consideration of this Bill went on until 2.21am and the House actually rose at 4.02am, the job was done.

In the early hours, or the late hours, as the remainder of the proceedings was inconsequentially drawing to a close, we sat around in the all-male[2] Whips Office rather as you might see in a wartime film of young fighter pilots after a successful mission at Biggin Hill. Except we were older and maybe a bit more dissolute. Ashtrays were piled high, papers were strewn. An empty bottle on the floor. The signs of considerable and continued drinking, jackets off, ties down, shirts unbuttoned, maybe the odd shoe off and a general sense of exhaustion and profound relief in the fug of the Office.

There was a knock at the door. No one moved or cared. A rebel coming to apologise? Well if it was we could jeer or tell him to f*** off or we could pour him a drink. The options were all ours now.

But it wasn't a rebel. It was the Prime Minister. In spite of the hour, Margaret Thatcher looked as if it was lunchtime and she was dressed for a cocktail party. Her hair was beautiful. I think now, though I hadn't time to

---

1. Tristan Garel-Jones M.P. (Watford) now Lord Garel-Jones. 2. As it was then.

think then, of President Mitterand's description of her as 'Marilyn Monroe with the eyes of Caligula'. In the idiom of Biggin Hill, we scrambled! In a few seconds of flurry, ties were tied, shoes laces too, jackets on, bottles hidden, the contents of ashtrays jettisoned in to waste bins, papers gathered. Stand up, for God' sake, stand. She eased into our midst serenely and magnetically. David Lightbown[3] had had the presence of mind to pour her a large whisky in a huge tumbler. We knew what she liked. David was the one to act on it. She accepted the drink as a matter of course and sank back into one of the sofas. Her skirt rode up showing us rather more of her very nice legs. She didn't adjust it. She put the glass to her lips and held it there. But her eyes travelled and engaged each one of us in eye contact for just that deliberate bit too long.

She sipped and then she said "I just wanted to thank you, boys".

The part of Margaret Thatcher was played by Marlene Deitrich or was it the other way round?

One of Marlene's immortal lines was "go see what the boys in the backroom will have and tell them I'm having the same".

We were Margarets' boys in the back room. She came and had one with us.

With these disciplines we ran a Conservative government for eighteen years. It was a tough regime but never an unfair one. But when wearied colleagues asked when they could go home the stock answer, the legendary Whips answer, was always PLEASE STAY TO THE ADJOURNMENT.

---

3. *The late Sir David Lightbown was M.P. for Lichfield & Tamworth.*

To my Mother and Father

Chapter 1

Air Raid Shelters - Part 1

"EX-ARMY CHAPLAIN (invalided after Dunkirk) SEEKS Country LIVING; Stipend unimportant - Write Box C328, The Times, EC4"

(An entry from the Personal Page of The Times on 19th August 1941, the day I was born. I shared 1941 with Operation Barbarossa, Pearl Harbour and the bombing of the House of Commons)

We had an air raid shelter in our garden. It had, as its roof, an upturned saucer of concrete 18 inches thick. My father had commissioned a local builder to build it. There were brick steps down into it, a pump to keep the water out and a power line from the house for electricity. I am told that I spent some time there in a carry-cot. I was also told by my mother that I made the noise "boom boom" when the bombs went off. We were 9 miles from Coventry, 10 miles from Birmingham and even nearer to Birmingham Airport and the Rover car plant in Solihull then known by the enemy to be devoted to the war effort.

In fact we received one very near miss which made a hole in the field next to our garden. I still have part of the casing of a German bomb, it may have been that one, which fell in Hampton. Father got it no doubt. Much more recently the County Architect, Alfie Wood, offered to have it expertly examined for me. I have been unable to find his letter but the result was that the bomb had been made in Dusseldorf and I once had the batch number. There is a curious story about the bomb which may have been an incendiary which did not go off properly because my father said he would use the end of a trowel to take a little of the substance that remained in it as a very effective fire lighter. Meanwhile the blackout was enforced by the village policeman, P.C. Lindley, whose front bicycle lamp was blacked at the top of its glass, presumably his own contribution to the blackout.

I had a gas mask which was red in colour and had a spatula nose to it through which I was to exhale. My parents' gas masks were bigger and black.

Father was in the Home Guard. I suppose it really was Dad's Army for me. I suspect it was sometimes funnier than Captain Mainwaring's outfit. It is said that they carried out plane spotting from the top of Hampton Church tower and on one occasion took up a large quantity of Brown Ale which

Please Stay To The Adjournment

would have been either from the White Lion or just possibly from the Ring O'Bells pub which may then still have been open.

The Brown Ale could have done little for the plane spotting and in the end they had to be helped down.

There was one piece of real live action, so the memory goes, of a small German plane coming down between Eastcote and Barston, which would certainly be visible from Hampton Church tower, and of the pilot surrendering to the Home Guard who had rushed to the scene. It is hard to imagine who was more frightened, but they took him to the American Barracks at Packington which seemed the right thing to do.

Talking of Americans, the instruction came round the village that households would have to make arrangements to accommodate American soldiers and make ready for inspection such rooms as could be spared. My parents had the good sense to make the best bedroom and the front living room available. In consequence there were billeted at our house two really nice young officers called Ken Cahoon and Jim Edmister who supplemented mother's wartime food rations quite handsomely. They exchanged news and Christmas cards with us for years and years afterwards. Incidentally, those who made less generous space available or poorer rooms got less good guests.

I don't know when it was but I can remember American tanks coming through Hampton and people waving and the American soldiers throwing chewing gum packets and Ping-Pong balls to them. Why Ping-Pong balls I have no idea. The tanks cracked the paving stones if they left the road, and went on to the pavement. I do know that. I saw it.

We also had Italian prisoners of war working on at least one local farm, Patrick's Farm. The local girls tittered about these "Eyeties".

The saddest story I have to say is not remembered by me directly. I feel as if I was aware of it but I can only really know what my mother told me.

In the early and worst stages of the bombing people would come out from Birmingham into the lanes and villages to escape the terror. Sometimes they would come to the door and ask for water. After one such occasion, father apparently said "We'll let the next ones stay". So it was that Mr and Mrs Berry from Small Heath, in inner Birmingham, came to stay with us. They had a young daughter called Mary. She had been so terrified that for quite some time she could not speak.

As with our American service guests, Christmas cards were exchanged with this family for many years.

Towards the end of the war, I think it must have been in 1945, father took me to see Coventry. He knew me as well as in later life I was to know

Chapter One – Air Raid Shelters - Part 1

him. He thought I was a bright impressionable, if sensitive, little boy and he wanted me to see a smashed City. Not for fun, quite the reverse. It was a pattern that was to be repeated as I got older. He would deliberately take me to see things and make no comment, allowing me to think about them for myself. He wanted me to see Coventry and remember it. I do. I can close my eyes and see it now 58 years later. The central block all the way down to Pool Meadow was destroyed. Few bricks were left standing on any other bricks. There were duckboards and planks and mud and hosepipes and a curious little exhibition to remind us that our soldiers were still fighting, in the Far East, Burma I think. Perhaps that would date it between VE Day and VJ Day. (Incidentally, Coventry, before the Blitz, had more old buildings than Warwick and was considered by some people to be more attractive too.)

I enjoyed VE Day with all the flags and bunting and it was a fine weather day in Hampton and I had my photograph taken in front of the name plaque on the front wall of our house, "Meadside", with a union flag hanging from it.

By VJ Day I had a little brother, Michael. Later we would play together in our air raid shelter. But not for very long. It began to flood. The place of safety from aerial bombardment had itself become dangerous.

Chapter 2

Air Raid Shelters - Part 2

*Adapted from an item by the author in the
Solihull Times of Friday 30 July 1999.*

I went to this barbecue in Dovehouse Lane on a recent Saturday evening.

The interesting thing was that a fair number of the houses at the lower end of Dovehouse Lane on the odd numbered side had air raid shelters in their gardens.

I was told that the title deeds made it clear that the air raid shelters were part of the specification or, at the very least, an optional extra when the houses were originally built in 1938.

In 1938? As one born in 1941, that tells me something that I had not fully appreciated. It tells me, better than any historian could, that, at least a year before we entered the Second World War, a Solihull housebuilder and people seeking houses in Solihull, one as the seller and the others as buyers, decided that air raid shelters were seriously worth having.

Whatever they were being told about 'peace in our time' these Solihull people had other ideas. Grimly, of course, they were right.

Chapter 3

Lancashire

*My Brother's Birth - Rice Pudding -
Hollingworth Lake - "Patience"*

Whereas I am personally essentially a child of Hampton-in-Arden and Solihull, I have to relate myself to the fact that both my parents were Lancastrians who settled in Hampton-in-Arden, in their first married home, in 1935.

I hardly knew my father's parents but I certainly knew my mother's parents. They were known to me as Grandad and Granny. Grandad was to be a benign influence on my formative life. In his retirement he presided over a settled regime of which he was the central figure. He had wound down his own business in the late 1930s, followed the Second World War with maps and bulletins at his disposal and was an extraordinarily well read late Victorian. He could quote vast quantities of Tennyson and Byron. He had his own views on the Church of England. He was a Tory. He had been Chairman of Milnrow Urban District Council and a Magistrate and chairman of the local hospital board and other such things. He was prodigiously a walker, not least to and around Hollingworth Lake, and a prodigious reader too and a prominent member of the local Literary and Scientific Society. He was at the same time both scarcely educated by others but superbly educated by himself.

Born, as he was, in the age of horse-drawn transport, he and I watched the first moon landing together on television.

He was one of the funniest men I ever met. At his seventieth birthday he held a party, dominated by himself, at which he spoke to his assembled friends and, at which, for the only time in my life, I fell out of my chair with laughter.

It was with these grandparents that I was sent to stay when my brother was born in 1945. Lunch in their home was always early. The lunchtime news on the radio came on at 1.00pm. By then we would have reached the pudding stage of lunch. This was always rice pudding.

Grandad would turn on the wireless, as we would then have called it, tuned to the Home Service and we would all listen to the news. This is how I came, forever afterwards, to associate BBC English with rice pudding. During this same period my grandmother had cause to rebuke me for impatience. She said "John, have patience!" It is said that I replied "No thank you Granny, I don't like a patience". Nor did I. Nor do I still.

Some days after my brother's birth which occurred on 31 July 1945, my parents telephoned to consider arrangements for my return home. By then I did not want to go home. I was happy where I was so I made my own indefinite terms for remaining. I told my father I wished to stay with my grandparents for another ten days. It was as long as I could think of. It was also an act of defiance but my wish was granted.

Chapter 4

Eversfield School

"Et mea messis erit"
(and my harvest shall be ...)
Learning about trying; learning about unfairness.

I went to Eversfield Preparatory School in Solihull in September 1946 at the age of five. I cried on my first day ascending the stairs to the kindergarten leaving my parents behind. This despite the fact that I knew I would be going there and had told my parents that I was looking forward to it. I sat next to Geoffrey Pollard and Peter Derrington. From time to time I have been in random contact with them ever since. Geoffrey Pollard was involved in Solihull Round Table in later years and Peter Derrington became a local dentist.

Eversfield was a religious school, low Church of England one might say, and three of the senior masters were ordained. Two of them were bachelors. There was the Reverend Peacock (the Head, in my time), the Reverend Coleman and the Reverend Hill. I told my grandfather about this and he said "I think you need a rev. counter". (Schoolboy humour for my benefit). I never knew any of these men's first names. I still don't. Anyway to me they were all "Sir". To them I was "Taylor J." until the arrival of my brother Michael whereupon I became "Taylor 1" and he was, from the start, "Taylor 2".

Memory works at different levels. On the one hand, perhaps rather uncharitably or even unfairly, and with an element of boyish defiance, there is the recollection of some rather odd masters and some contrastingly sympathetic mistresses. There is the clearest memory of prayers, which we certainly took seriously, and an even more vivid awareness of "the whack" as the ultimate punishment which could be administered to us. This took the form of blows on the bare buttock with a slipper. Parental permission did not seem to be required or may have been given by parents in advance as a condition of admission to the school. I experienced this twice. Once at the hands of Mr Peacock, for not finishing some Latin homework, and once at the hands of Mr Hill for what I cannot remember. I have no strong recollection as to whether I thought either was just or unjust. Both upset me.

That is remembering Eversfield at one level.

However, 50 years has passed, half a century, and enormous social changes have taken place over that time. Given a serious retrospective effort to judge Eversfield by the standards of the 1940's and 1950's and, with whatever lingers of boyish puffery stripped away, a rather different picture emerges. Here was an absolutely dedicated institution, founded on Christian principles, devoted to the task of producing a 13 year old end product who would be god-fearing, smartly turned out, respectful of his elders, scholarly to his very maximum personal potential, physically fit and, if possible, possessed of prowess on the games field. I sincerely believe that these objectives were pursued for their own virtue. But there was of course also an end product to be delivered to the fee paying parents: success in the Common Entrance examination which gave admission to the Public School of the parents' choice. As this climax approached, those thought to be scholarship material, of which I was one, were separately groomed but never with any sense of favouritism. For those few boys whom Mr Peacock and his senior staff (I presume) considered unlikely to pass the Common Entrance, Mr Peacock, doubtless with the concurrence of the parents, found alternative destinations which might perhaps be academically less demanding but nonetheless entirely suitable for the boy in question. In this I give great credit to Mr Peacock on at least two counts. First, looking after the separate arrangements for these boys was done with such discretion that none of the rest of us were aware of it. There was no stigma against them just as there was no favouritism for scholarship candidates. In these respects, as in many others at Eversfield, the regime which surrounded us, was egalitarian and even handed. If I have described correctly what Eversfield was trying to achieve then I have to say it was triumphantly successful. Nor can I believe that anybody made much money out of the school as a business.

An incident lingers from my penultimate year. I would have been 12. Playing for the school in a cricket match against another team I made a score of 28. I should explain that with the wickets we played on and given the attention span of boys of 12, a team total of 70 or 80 was often good enough to win a match. So it was that 28 was considered a good personal score. At least our cricket master, Mr Trotman, thought so and he told me, rather to my surprise, that if I could do as well again in the next match I would be awarded my cricket colours. I do not think that this prospect had seriously entered my head until he said it. I think I thought that cricket colours were very desirable. I am not sure that I had ever thought of myself as a likely candidate and, certainly, no one had ever offered so clear a prescription for how to achieve them.

The next match was to be at Stoneygate Prep School in Leicester. What Mr Trotman had told me was never out of my mind. When we batted I was

Chapter Four – Eversfield School

soon at the crease. I batted with immense determination, at least all the determination that I could muster, and concentrated on every ball that I faced. I made 30. A few days later I was awarded my school cricket colours. I do not recount this story vaingloriously or to parade that I had the beginnings of some modest aptitude for cricket. It is a much deeper lesson than that which has stayed with me. It was a lesson learned about trying. A lesson that not all the prizes were necessarily to the most gifted but that some would go to those who tried hard enough. There may have been other episodes which had given me a glimpse of this but never anything so obvious, or so simply illustrative of the connection between the effort and the prize.

I also learned another thing, quite to my surprise, that when the master responsible for PT (Physical Training) got my entire class to run to the far side of the Eversfield games field and back, quite a long way, I found it relatively effortless to come second to a boy who was already an acknowledged athlete considered likely to win the Victor Ludorum on Sports Day, still to come.

Until then I had no idea that I had the potential to become a long distance runner.

In my final year at Eversfield, aged thirteen, I had an enjoyable final cricket season. I scored my first fifty as a batsman and took 6-15 against Coventry Prep. School including dismissing, first ball, the youngest of three cricketing Richardson brothers. Both of his older brothers went on to play for England. P.E. (Peter) Richardson played for England over thirty times as an opening batsman with some distinction. D.W. Richardson played once for England, in the same side as Peter, in 1957 in the Edgbaston Test against the West Indies, an occasion at which I was present as a teenage spectator.

At the prize giving immediately before I left, at the end of my final term (of which more later), I was awarded the Bowling Cup and the ceremonial bat for the Best All-Round Cricketer as well as the Cup for the Runner Up to the Victor Ludorum. All of which was gratifying.

I have said all along that Eversfield's was a fair regime, and yet, at the last, it was to give me an insight into unfairness. I cannot say that by the age of 13 I did not realise that life could be unfair. Of course I did. But the Prize giving at the end of my final term at Eversfield was to give me a poignant jolt. The ultimate prize in the School, in those days at any rate, was the Proficiency Cup, which the Headmaster always described as being for the "best all round boy". It was conventional, if slightly curious, that a short list of two boys was announced at least a term, if not longer than that, ahead of the award. I was one of the two. You'll have gathered that I didn't get it. I would not have minded very much or even at all if I had felt that it was obviously a close thing between me and my rival. But it wasn't.

It was, I thought, unfair. It is true that I had already received three prizes. By contrast, he had received none. But he was an early example of an overseas student from a wealthy background and was on his way to Westminster School, which was a prestigious graduation from Eversfield. Maybe fairness was sharing things around?

In isolation, this personal experience would be insufficient to suggest that Eversfield, or the Headmaster, had an agenda for Prize giving. After all the Head may have found a character defect in me which he had never seen fit to draw to my attention and marked me down on that. But 4 years later my bother Michael, who had been outstandingly the School's best cricketer in his final year, was awarded, irresistibly, on runs scored and wickets taken, both the batting cup and the bowling cup. There was a third and final award for cricket which was for The Best All-Round Cricketer. Michael did not get that. It went to somebody else with a vastly inferior record. Since Michael was also the best fielder, a good team "man" and the captain, there can be absolutely no explaining his experience.

In 1991, the School's Diamond Jubilee, I was invited to Eversfield's Open Day and Award Ceremony, as MP for Solihull and as an Old Boy, and handed out the prizes myself. They were passed to me by the Headmaster, naturally enough. They included the Bowling Cup, the award for the Best All-Round Cricketer and of course the Proficiency Cup.

Chapter 5

An Interlude On Ancient Monuments

Adapted from the author's article in The House Magazine of 5 December 1988, part of a series of contributions entitled "Hobby Horse" in which M.P.s wrote about their other interests.

I was born in the Warwickshire village of Hampton-in-Arden. The parish church which dominates the village is as old as Doomsday. At least in part. The village itself has a substantial entry in the Doomsday Book. It must have been a long established settlement when the Normans came. I think I grasped as a young boy that people had lived in my village for more than a thousand years and I know that I was curious and interested.

My initial instruction in history at school began with 1066 as I suppose it did for many of us. But there was an earlier chapter in my elementary book which illustrated the Old Stone Age, New Stone Age, the Bronze Age and the Iron Age. I found it fascinating. My abiding interest is in ancient monuments generally and the great stone monuments in particular. The megaliths. I disclaim any level of scholarship in this hobby. I am an enthusiast. A romantic rather than an expert.

We had holidays in Cornwall when I was young. My late father, with whom we had a very easy and happy relationship, showed my brother and me an ancient Iron Age village called Carn Euny, an Iron Age headland hill fort known as Maen Castle, high above Sennen Cove, a great stone disc on three stone uprights called Lanyon's Quoit and the 'Merry Maidens', a stone circle. On return from one of our visits to Sennen, father made a detour. He showed us a far greater thing. He showed us Stonehenge. As the years have gone by, no holiday has been complete for me without seeing local antiquities.

Some scholars say that the impulse of megalithic construction came from the Eastern Mediterranean and travelled north and westward. Certainly the first Stonehenge is thought to be contemporary with the beginning of the Middle Minoan period. In recent years I have been able to travel a little more in the Mediterranean. My visit to Knossos on Crete was a pilgrimage. Likewise to Delphi in a different sense and on another occasion. The Taulas of Minorca were a fascinating surprise. These huge and spectacular 'T' shaped constructions consist of one vast upright stone and another almost as large across the top of it. In an eight day holiday in Minorca, unprepared for discovering them and with a local map that carried only a general symbol for antiquities, I found and photographed five of them. Four could be said to be intact. In the limited archaeological section of my guidebook I came across the speculation that the manpower required to erect them would have accounted for a significant proportion of the population of the island as it then must have been. I can believe it. As so often there was no clear idea of their purpose. Altars for human sacrifice cannot be excluded, I suspect.

Nearer home, the Stones of Stenness and Ring of Brogda on Orkney are splendid specimens in my photographic records as are the superb Standing Stones of Callanish on Lewis in the Outer Hebrides. There is a point to this. The remoter the site by reference to more modern civilization, the better preserved these monuments tend to be. Subsequent primitive, survival agriculture would have regarded standing stones as obstructions. Religious views have been hostile at times to ancient paganism. Thus the damage at Avebury.

There are no megaliths in Solihull but the struggle has been a real one, first to protect a Saxon earthwork called the Mount and recently to recover medieval Hobs Moat from neglect and erosion. Distress to ancient monuments can be most intense amid the pressures of suburbia. Twentieth century vandalism takes many forms. Every year we have a crisis at Stonehenge, the local Member knows this all too well, as drop-out people in their weird convoys threaten possession. Less obvious is the fact that more orthodox enthusiasts erode these precious sites too. Did you know that as recently as the 1930's hammers were for sale in Salisbury for admirers to knock their own souvenir chunks off Stonehenge?

There is, of course, no shortage of support for various theories about the origins and meaning of stone circles in Britain. In some cases, as we know, the monuments are aligned to the solstices with a remarkable, obviously deliberate, geometric precision. It is open to any of us to speculate whether they are temples, sacrificial theatres, primitive observatories, timekeepers of the rituals and seasons, or all of these. But I suspect megaliths are something more besides. Prestige and pride, arrogance even, is inherent in them. To me they represent the beginnings of the assertion of modern man. Bronowski might have called it presumption. He spoke in those terms at the excavated base of a tower (nine thousand years old) in Jericho in his magnificent television production *The Ascent of Man*. A great deal of self-confidence and self-belief must have been necessary as well as planning, determination and collective and, most likely, coerced exertion. Megalithic man assessed the difficulties and considered the odds. Then he defied them. That is part of the magnificence of these monuments.

Chapter Five – An Interlude On Ancient Monuments

Meanwhile the megalithic civilisation left no writing which adds an element of romantic mystery to the wonder of it; they must have had a big idea but we can only imagine what it might have been.

Post Script

Not long after writing this original article I visited Brittany and in particular Carnac where are to be found perhaps the most famous of the 'Alignments'. This is an awesome megalithic arrangement comprising several extended parallel rows of upright standing stones called Menhirs. In fact there are 2,935 of these standing stones and their parallel rows extend over some three kilometres. I think it would be fair to say that Carnac is to alignments what Stonehenge is to stone circles.

Brittany is a neolithic field of treasure, studded with Menhirs, Cromlechs and Dolmen, its landscape rippled with earthworks.

In 1993 I visited Petra in Jordan. Petra is a monument to the Nabataean civilization. Their breathtaking dwellings and temples are characterized by magnificent elevations carved on rock faces with their interiors hewn into the rock behind.

I made what is almost always a mistake as I walked down the two mile long siq (or canyon), meandering, winding and narrowing with its sides rising higher above me, to see Petra. I allowed my expectations to soar. But even with the highest sense of anticipation, I was utterly unprepared for what confronted me when I got there. The carved "Treasury" elevation was suddenly upon me. One of the most remarkable things I have ever seen in my life.

I draw these comments to a close with a curiosity that struck me on my trip to Egypt in 1992. Apart from a brief visit to Cairo, I was based in Luxor. I visited the Valley of the Kings and the superb temple up-river at Dendera. But perhaps the high spot was the temple of Rameses the Second at Karnak. I was puzzled by the word "Karnak". I asked the guide if it was an Arab word. He said it was not and that he was not sure of its derivation.

Given that much early Egyptology, with its attendant excavation, was carried out by French archaeologists in Napoleonic times, I have wondered ever since if this was a scholarly and whimsical French word-play left behind by these archaeologists, its origin lost in the meantime.

Is it not possible that these French archaeologists in Egypt, first encountering these massive, half buried, stone structures by the Nile nicknamed them by reference to their own greatest monumental antiquity? Is Karnak a simulation of Carnac?

Chapter 6

Bromsgrove School

"Floreat Bromsgrovia"
(May Bromsgrove flourish)

John Freeman was probably my father's best friend at the time. They were respectively Captain and Secretary of Hampton-in-Arden Cricket Club. John Freeman had been to Bromsgrove. Father, who had not been brought up in the Midlands, did not have a better idea. So I went to Bromsgrove in Worcestershire. So did four others from Eversfield at the same time.

Bromsgrove was a very pleasant market town. Well it still is but it has put on a bit of girth since I was a pupil there from 1955 to 1960.

The oldest of the school's buildings are very much part of the town with a frontage onto the Worcester Road. But to the east of these earlier buildings there opens out a quite magnificent quadrangle of more modern buildings surrounding a large Green intersected by tree-lined paths. These buildings included the Headmaster's house, School House, the Old Chapel, the gymnasium, Gordon House, the Science Laboratories, and an imposing classroom building called Kyteless. The quadrangle is completed by the Memorial Chapel, originally dedicated to Bromsgrovians who had been killed in the First World War, and an Assembly Hall called Routh Hall named after Bromsgrove's greatest Headmaster, R.G. Routh.

To the south of this there extend magnificent playing fields, known as Charford, culminating at their furthest extent in a beautifully proportioned cricket pavilion, itself modelled on the pavilion at Worcester's lovely County Ground but to a smaller scale.

To "R.G." must forever be the credit for this whole superb layout.

Whilst it is stated in a Charter granted to Bromsgrove by Queen Mary in 1556 "that a Grammar School had existed in Bromsgrove from time immemorial", [1] the history of the modern Bromsgrove School can authentically be traced to 1693 and the far sighted benefaction of Sir Thomas Cookes. He is properly regarded as the Founder of the School and Commemorated as such once a year. He was a man of some significance because he was also the founder of Worcester College, Oxford, which incidentally has an identical coat of arms to that of Bromsgrove School.

But there is another man who perhaps can rival even Cookes and Routh in Bromsgrove's gratitude. Routh's successor, D.J. Walters, was Headmaster

1. *Bromsgrove School Through Four Centuries by HEM Icely.*

Chapter Six – Bromsgrove School

when the whole school was requisitioned by the Government during the Second World War and occupied by "the Tank Board, and later sections of the India Office and of the Ministry of Supply". [2] Walters had the massive task of evacuating the school to Llanwrtyd Wells in central Wales and of keeping it going throughout that time without all his young school masters gone to war, presumably replaced, as best could be, by older men or men brought out of retirement. Then he had the equally great task of bringing it back again to Bromsgrove. All this whilst holding onto that "critical mass" of pupils with fee paying parents without which, I suspect, the school itself might have become a casualty of war.

For this enduring achievement, Walters is rightly held in affectionate memory as one of the most honoured in the Bromsgrove Pantheon.

The school, when I went there, was all boys and almost all boarding, with a few day boys. I was to be a boarder. I had boarded, in familiar surroundings, for my last year at Eversfield. So, while there were many new things and new people to get used to, boarding itself was not a new experience.

A herringbone suit, to a particular specification, was the school's uniform and there were strict rules as to which of various school ties a boy was supposed to wear. For the first term a black tie was compulsory.

Then, after that, you could wear a plain red one. After two years you could wear a tie in the colours of your House. Far into the hopeful future, at times it seemed like the hopeless future, there would be prestigious ties indicating that you had been awarded House or even School colours for notable sporting achievement. A long way off for a new boy.

My general memory of Bromsgrove is happy and amusing and approving but, if I am really careful in my memory, I think my first year was miserable. We had a fagging regime at Bromsgrove, though not called by that name, and in my first year I bore my share of the brunt of it and I also had a reputation for being a swot, never a fashionable thing to be. But the swot was to re-sit the scholarship examination internally and won an exhibition worth £45 a year, subsequently up-rated to £80, at a time when the annual fees, payable by my father, were £200. This, as I now know, made a big difference to my parents who were already accepting financial help from my grandparents on my mother's side to keep me at Bromsgrove. During this year too I made my nervous debut in the Junior Debating Society. This was to be more important than I could have known at the time.

But there was an awkward thing. Very early on in this experience there was a debate in the School's Junior Debating Society on a subject chosen for us by more senior people. We were only boys, after all. I was no more

2. *Bromsgrove School Through Four Centuries* by HEM Icely.

than fourteen years old. It was about apartheid. I chose to speak on what would now be regarded as the hopelessly ill-advised side of the argument. In my nervous innocence, all those years ago, I thought you could take a contrary view, as a challenge, if nothing else. After all, if nobody did, then the debate simply wouldn't happen. At the end of the debate a vote was taken and the "wrong" side won. My side. Even now I must admit the possibility that, notwithstanding the immaturity of all the participants, maybe our side spoke better!

Anyway the School Chaplain "Black Jack" Cunningham went round every Divinity lesson in School "preaching" against me. With the benefit of maturity I am sure he was right. But I am also sure, in a way, he was wrong. Debating Societies, surely, are for people to try their ideas and try their skills. The most generous interpretation that I can put on all of this is that the authorities that supervised the Junior Debating Society were right to let us debate apartheid and the School Chaplain was right to denounce the result. Even so it was pretty bewildering for a fourteen year old. I composed a letter to the School magazine, "The Bromsgrovian", but I never sent it.

At the end of my first year, in the summer term, I was awarded my Junior Colts colours for cricket in front of the whole school. There were six of us rewarded in this way. Memory plays good tricks. A lot of the rest of that first year is forgotten or subliminally buried.

My second year followed a rather similar pattern and had its disappointments. But I got my Colts colours for cricket and reasonably good 'O' Level results in the General Certificate of Education (GCE) which put me into the Sixth Form for my next and third year.

I can only say that my third year was better to the point of being neutral. The balance between misery and enjoyment was about equal. It was the transition between the small boy juniority of the first two years and the best, which was still to come. I was a Sixth Former now, studying Maths and Physics. I was a two-year "man", able to wear my House tie but I did not make the school 1st XI at cricket and I played rather disappointedly in the 2nd XI. The 1st XI was very strong. I knew that in other years I would have got into the 1st XI myself.

The year 1959, after one term of my fourth year, was the turnaround. I was now 17 years old. On the 2nd January I took my driving test in Leamington Spa in my father's car. After my test the examiner told my waiting father all the things I needed to improve. Father and I listened disconsolately. Then the examiner took the "L" plates off the car and told me I had passed. It was theatrical but ultimately done with kindness. Going back to school for the Easter Term with a driving licence was a "manhood

Chapter Six – Bromsgrove School

token" in an adolescent world. I knew it and so did my contemporaries who had also passed or, just as likely, failed. That Easter Term was the term for Hockey but, more importantly for me, it was also the term for cross-country running.

Bromsgrove School had a strong record in cross-country running. This may owe something to the years of wartime exile in Wales when other sport and games would have been difficult to organise if only for the lack of pitches and of young school masters. It is probably no coincidence that the trophy awarded for the annual inter-House cross country competition at Bromsgrove School is called the Llanwrtyd Wells Cup.

The standard course in my day was six miles. Our run was called "The Canal" because part of its course was the towpath of the great "Tardebigge Steps" flight of locks on the Birmingham to Worcester Canal. In the inter-House final, teams of five from each of six houses competed, a field of thirty. I came fifth and was awarded my House Colours (another tie) for Cross-Country Running. By now I was competing successfully in the School Cross-Country Running Eight and very soon afterwards I won my School Colours (another tie). Ties were important.

Then came the summer term. I made the cricket 1st XI at last. I bowled well and topped the bowling averages. I got my School Colours for cricket. I didn't bat badly either. I got a 50 batting in our House Match with Millington House and was awarded my House Colours for cricket. This was an ambition, long sought, but frankly, only then deserved. I was very aware that I had not previously played well enough in House Matches.

It was also the year I sat my 'A' Level examinations for the first time and got a modestly good result. Two 'A' Levels, as I recall, but there was going to be another year at Bromsgrove.

Two observations about education before that, both devoid of rancour. The first is that your examination results can be hugely dependent on who teaches you and their style. Where I had good teachers I did well. Where I had bad teachers I did less well. To this day I can remember being taught Latin up to 'O' Level by Joe Carson. Hannibal had come down through the Alps and had smashed the Roman Legions at Cannae. Quintus Fabius made a desperate, rousing, speech in the Senate. He was given command and somehow reassembled the Legions. Then he developed his tactics of delay and feint, harassing Hannibal, but never risking battle.

What a way to teach Latin, all animation and shouting! ("In the voice of forty thousand foghorns", was Joe Carson's own description of his teaching technique). I can remember it now over 40 years later. I had rather a good examination result in Latin!

If only I could have had a similar teacher of French with a set book about Napoleon's campaigns and another Joe Carson roaring at us about Austerlitz and Marengo and the river crossings on the Retreat from Moscow, how well I might have learnt French in such circumstances.

How differently I was taught French in fact. It was all about Monsieur Lepine and his son Toto having cornflakes for their breakfast before Toto went to school and his father went to work via the local railway station. It is true that towards the end of my formal instruction in French we were introduced to a little Moliere but that apart there was no inspiration in my learning of French provided either by teacher or by text and I regret it.

My other educational observation, is this. If you are going to be deeply involved in sport whilst you are a student - don't be a cricketer. All the most important exams are held in the summer. I was a cricketer and I have no regrets about that. But I believe my exam results might in every case have been better had they been sat in any other part of the year.

So to my final year at Bromsgrove. By now I was a monitor (prefect). I was to become School Captain of cross-country running, I was to be "capped" for cricket, topping the bowling averages again. There were unusually economic bowling figures in the match against King's School Worcester of 14-11-5-2. There were only three scoring shots made off my bowling in those fourteen overs. There were also useful figures against Oakham School of 8-63 and 3-12 in a two innings match on Charford.

I was Secretary of the Debating Society.

I had played the part of Knowledge in the morality play 'Everyman', the school play.

I was to get 'A' Levels results in Maths, Physics and Applied Mechanics good enough subsequently to admit me to Birmingham University.

Through this time, as a boarder at Bromsgrove, I was playing golf at nearby Blackwell Golf Club on Sunday afternoons quite regularly. Boys from the School could do so for a mere two shillings a round, quite a privilege on such a splendid course.

I knew how favourable this green fee was. It would be churlish to say I took advantage of it; fairer to say I appreciated it. We would also play with masters from the School from time to time and had an annual match against them in which I played. I had a keen match with the Bursar one year and in another I halved with Don Gibbin, Wendron's House Tutor, even though he had had me five down with five to play.

Early in my final year there was a General Election. It was on 8th October 1959. I would be eighteen years old and I was the monitor (prefect) in charge of a bedder (dormitory) of lively sixteen year olds. I took a radio

Chapter Six – Bromsgrove School

to bed with me and listened to the results as they came in. Those results would have come in earlier than they do today because the polls then closed at 9 o'clock at night. "...the first results began to come in soon after 10.00pm ...".[3] That would be not long after "lights out" in our bedder.

Although I rather thought I was a Liberal at the time, just to be different, I remember being very satisfied that the Conservatives were clearly winning. But perhaps a much more important recollection, and an enduring one, is that I was clearly much more interested in the result of the Election than any of the other boys. Not for the first time, I had acquired a piece of self-knowledge of which I had been previously unaware.

A happier memory of the Debating Society was the occasion when, billed as Sir John Taylor QC, I defended Field Marshal Montgomery against charges of war crimes. The prosecution was led by John Grice (of whom more later in our subsequent legal careers). "Monty" was played, very sportingly, by that most splendid of Bromsgrove's teachers of my time, John Hedley, who had a very distinguished war in the Far Eastern campaign. "Jungle Jim", as we called him, played his part perfectly and when he was acquitted he strode across our mock court-room in the Old Chapel to shake my hand and thank me and congratulate me for his successful defence.

My cricketing finale was a happy one. I left the field at the end of our final fixture, which was drawn, with my best school friend Don Amphlet, both of us not out. It was symbolic. We had finished that part of our lives.

At about the same time, at the very end of my final year at Bromsgrove, I was told that I had been proposed and seconded and invited to join the Bromsgrove Martlets. This was a rather privileged Old Boys Cricket Club in that usually only retiring 'capped' members of the 1st XI, of which I was one, were invited to join. It was the best leaving present I could possibly have had.

It was traditional to take one's leave of the Headmaster when leaving School. I had not been close to Lionel Carey but I had no reason to dislike him. Indeed he had involved me in a rather elite "Semi-Circle" for which I had written an essay for discussion about Dictators including the ingredient elements of their rise to power. Luck was an important factor, I concluded. I think he rather approved. He was a man of few words. At our parting he took his pipe out of his mouth, smiled, extended his hand and said "Well bowled Taylor".

I left Bromsgove.

In 1983 I was guest speaker at Commemoration as a newly elected MP and as an Old Bromsgrovian.

In 1993, the Tercentenary of Sir Thomas Cookes' Foundation, I was to become President of the Old Bromsgrovian Club.

3. *The Times Guide to the House of Commons 1959.*

Chapter 7

A Set Back (1960 - 61)

The year in which I achieved nothing, went backwards: an insight into failure

So I went to university modestly decorated as a cricketer, modestly equipped as a scholar and certainly, if I may say, well read for my age. I was cocky, only superficially self confident and uncertainly urging for girls.

Looking back on it all, I would have benefited from what is now called a 'gap year'. National Service would have been even better, especially if I could have had a commission. After all I had passed Certificate A Parts 1 and 2 (based on the British Infantry Manual) relatively early on in my five years in the "Corps" [1] at Bromsgrove and went on to instruct the younger boys as most of us did. But during my time at Bromsgrove, National Service was ended for boys born like me in 1941.

I was in this uncertain age of adolescence [2]. My subsequent sympathy with this state of male development was to help me in the future in my representation in court of so many male youths before magistrates. Many of the male magistrates might be relied upon to recall their own adolescence but any of the magistrates, men or women, through their more recent experience as parents, could reasonably be relied upon to have similar experiences or bruises or insights through their own children.

I set out to study Civil Engineering at Birmingham University. CIV ENG., as it was known. The faculty was prestigious not least because of Professor Kolbuszewski, an intolerant genius.

Almost from the start my heart was not in it. Any extra mural activity was more interesting. But I made some good friends including John Redman, who subsequently became a client of my law practice, and Peter Hinchliffe for whom I subsequently became best man (the first of six times I was best man) and to whose daughter, Alice, I subsequently became godfather.

Quite early on in the year John Betjeman spoke at lunch time to the Students Union. He gave an elegant talk about furniture. I asked him how he would put a television set in a period room. Surprisingly he had no answer. Probably he should have said that he wouldn't have a TV in a period room. But he didn't.

On another occasion, a Conservative party meeting, I remember saying that I was a communist and making some difficulty for them. This was mad and baseless. The need to draw attention to myself was probably born of insecurity.

---

1. *The enduring name of the O.T.C. (Officers Training Corps) even though it had been renamed the Combined Cadet Force before I was involved in it.* 2. *"...that contemptuous time in most young men's life" (Christopher Sykes' biography of Evelyn Waugh).*

Chapter Seven – A Set Back (1960 - 1961)

My whole experience at Birmingham University was probably all about insecurity, uncertainty, exuberance and bravado. The shock was to come and I was to fail. I received the news after playing in a cricket match while we were on a field survey in Brockhampton. The match had been arranged between us, the University survey team, and the local village team. I took a hat trick, all bowled. Characteristically, in this set back year, I did well at the diversion not the main task in hand.

I was at University to get a degree in Civil Engineering.

I did not and events moved on.

I think I knew even then that I could get away with one failure. I also knew I could not get away with two.

On reflection, and in fairness to myself, it may be true to say that I had a romantic idea of civil engineering anyway. I was certainly fascinated by it and there were various episodes in my life when these had been brought home to me. In October 1952 there was an horrific train crash at Harrow and Wealdstone, described in O.S. Nock's [3] "Historic Railway Disasters" as "indescribably terrible". I was eleven and we had a television set. Reports from the scene showed the appalling wreckage. I was not unaware of the horror and deaths and tragedy, quite the reverse. But I remember being utterly absorbed by how the wreckage could be cleared, where to put the cranes and lifting gear and what an awesome challenge it represented to the engineer who was in charge of the operation. I wondered what it would have been like to have been him.

Even earlier as a young boy, more interested in the pictures than the text, I had been in the habit of borrowing from our local lending library in Hampton-in-Arden, books from the Wonder Book series. They would invariably be the Wonder Book of Railways or the Wonder Book of Bridges and the like. Throughout my boyhood, model railways, in particular, and Meccano construction sets had been an abiding indoor absorption to rival my intense interest in sports and games outside. I certainly had that interest, and still do, even though I ploughed my chance to become a qualified engineer myself, whether for reasons of adolescent instability or lack of aptitude, I will never know.

The final irony is that the decision to try to become an engineer was mine, partly influenced, I have no doubt, by the fact that my father was an engineer and it seemed to me to be a proper, manly occupation. The double irony is that my father himself had formed the view, before I was twelve, that I had the makings of a lawyer. He never pressed it upon me. That was not his way. But he was to live long enough to see me established in the legal profession and quite successfully so at that.

3. Copyright Ian Allan Ltd 1966.

Chapter 8

Aspirations

'Phoenix'

Peter Root was a good friend of my father's and he was also a good friend of mine. That might sound odd except that he was about half way between us in age. Hampton-in-Arden Cricket Club was our common interest, playing field and watering hole. Committee experience at Hampton-in-Arden Cricket Club and an introduction to how committees work and indeed how politics works had been, of itself, an initiation. One of the most important insights that I ever had.

Peter Root was an important man in my life not least because when my father told him that my university career in civil engineering had come to an end, Peter asked him if I might like to come and try the experience of working in a solicitors office. Peter was a partner in the firm of Reynolds & Co in Newhall Street, Birmingham. I had a momentary thought that I might be more tempted by a stockbrokers office. But that went no further. I shaved off my beard, pulled out the suit and a white shirt and reported for duty. This was a new environment and all my previous thoughts about becoming a civil engineer, an aspirant Brunel, designing suspension bridges or, more likely, me in a duffel coat supervising concrete culverts for sewers slipped away, I felt attracted by this solicitors office.

I had to decide what to call my principal when we were in the office because I called him Peter out of hours. Mr Root or even Sir would have been appropriate. But I found a comfortable solution by using the idiom of the Maigret programme, then very popular on television, and called him 'Patron' as Maigret's assistant called his boss. As it happened I was then in the habit of wearing a pork-pie hat rather like that of Maigret's assistant 'Lucas'. Anyway Peter Root responded in kind by calling me 'Lucas'. This was a happy, convenient and amusing arrangement.

I want to say the next things rapidly because they are about recovery from setback and they are important to me. Six weeks after joining Peter Root and Reynolds & Co I entered into Articles of Clerkship, the Solicitors' apprenticeship scheme, as it then was. Peter Root and I were signatories to the Deed of Articles and so was my father, because I was still under twenty one.

After fourteen months, in 1962, I had passed the Solicitors' Intermediate Examination on a correspondence course from the College of

Chapter Eight – Aspirations

Law. In 1964 I became Secretary of the Birmingham Law Students Society. In 1965 I took and passed my Solicitors' Final Examinations even as my father was in the Norwich & Norfolk hospital having had a heart attack. I had even prepared myself, as much as I could, for his death. I urged my mother into an hotel close to the hospital and spent the weekend before my finals revising the entire syllabus of the Solicitors' Finals alone in my parents' home in Wroxham. When I had concluded this round-the-clock revision, I took the train back to London. I sat the seven three-hour papers commencing on Monday morning and ending on Thursday lunchtime whereupon I went straight to my father's bedside from London as soon as the examinations were over. He was considerably recovered and in good spirits. I told him that I thought that I had passed my final exams.

On 2nd May 1966 I was, to give it its full resonance, admitted a Solicitor of the Supreme Court of Judicature. I have galloped this bit of my story because it reflects the essence of the urgency of my recovery and the immense amount of trying and effort that went into it. I had put myself back on track, not least in the sense of self-esteem and I knew it. This was also a crucial moment because I knew that a lot of my contemporaries who had achieved their professional qualification would probably think of no further ambition. I had other ideas and, even before my successful examination result had been made public, I anticipated it and wrote a letter to my father called 'Aspirations' in which I told him that my ambition was ultimately to head a law firm called 'John Taylor & Co' and thereafter to become a Member of Parliament. As I write this I have the satisfaction of having achieved both but I can never discount the contribution of an earlier failure to the attainment of those achievements. I drove myself. I worked so hard. Maybe I was looking back over my shoulder, determined never to fail again.

Quite separately, but during this time, a very beautiful female member of the staff of the firm, slightly older than me, taught me, outside office hours, the fun and ecstasy of grown-up sex beyond the fumbling and groping which was all that I had known before. I will be grateful to her forever. I send her my love wherever she is.

Chapter 9

An Interlude On Golf

"Golf may be played on Sunday, not being a game within the view of the law, but being a form of moral effort."
Stephen Butler Leacock, 1869 - 1944

Golf ranks second only after cricket in my deep personal affection for the sports and games which I have known and played. It also comes second only after cricket in terms of the literary quality and quantity of writing about any game. Numerous and significant golf writers, thorough in their knowledge and experience of the game and in their insight, include Bernard Darwin, Herbert Warren-Wind, Henry Longhurst and in lighter, humourous episodes such as PG Wodehouse. These and others have illuminated the game of golf with their writing.

What is it about this game that can be so club-throwingly, four-letter-wordedly, exasperating beyond any other game I have ever known and played? Not that you are supposed to yield to this exasperation, by the way. Above all you must behave and contain yourself on the golf course.

The answer may lie, not merely in the stunning setting of many golf courses but in the exquisite pleasure of a well hit long drive off the tee as the sensation comes up to the hands from the club head through the shaft and grip that you have as, Gene Sarazen said "nailed it".

Not much less is the sensation of a well hit sweeping shot off the fairway with a wood (these days paradoxically metal) or the chunky experience of punching an iron shot off the turf with a slightly more downward contact. Then there is the satisfaction of flopping a bunker shot lifeless a few inches from the hole.

Meanwhile, the better the golfer you are, the more it comes down to how well you can putt on the green. Nothing is more satisfying than the putt that drops nor more frustrating that the putt that stays out.

For just a few years I was actually quite a good golfer.

Father, though not himself a golfer, had secured junior membership of North Warwickshire Golf Club for me in my early teens for ten shillings a year. I must have expressed an interest. North Warwickshire Golf Club was about a mile and a half from our house and an easy bicycle ride for me with a few second hand ladies' clubs in a second hand "drainpipe" bag on my back.

Chapter Nine – An Interlude On Golf

My teenage golf was diversionary and unremarkable with the notable exception of a hole in one at the age of fifteen at the fifth hole at North Warwicks. This was a par three of about 155 yards. I hit the successful tee shot with a hickory shafted ladies five iron. My witness, playing with me, was my friend Tony Collett who went to both Eversfield and Bromsgrove with me. When the Captain of the Club got to hear about this he sent me a box of six golf balls and a letter of encouragement. It was a nice gesture and I hope I would have done the same if our roles had been reversed.

By the age of eighteen the game had become rather more than a school holiday diversion. I had become eligible to play in competitions at the Club and I was very keen to do so. I had to have a recognised handicap, of course. So I put in the necessary three marked cards and was given a handicap of eighteen. Pretty soon, winning monthly medals and monthly bogeys, as I did, my handicap came down to sixteen then fourteen then twelve then eleven then ten then nine and finally eight. My best handicap. And I could win competitions off it. This was an acquiring part of my manhood. It goes with my remarks about adolescence. I wanted to take on men on equal terms. I did and, sufficiently often, I beat them. I enjoyed the recognition. I wanted it.

The Radmore Cup, played match play, was regarded by North Warwickshire as the "Club Championship". In 1964 I reached the final. I had reached the semi final in the previous year. I was set to play this final over eighteen holes against Ron Miles. There were no strokes to be given or received. We were both off the same, single figure, handicap. I had had to hurry from work in central Birmingham to be on the course at the agreed time to tee off. The traffic had been awful and I had had an altercation with a motorcyclist. I arrived at the course badly rattled and with no time for any practice. None the less I hit a good drive off the first tee with a brand new ball which was fairly precious to me then on an articled clerk's pay. I went for the first green with my second shot, ambitiously with a nine iron and hit the ball half way up leaving it with a 'smile', as we used to say in those days, meaning a cut on the outer casing. But I didn't have another decent ball and so I played with it for the whole of the rest of the round. I lost the first three holes one after the other and was still three down after nine. We halved the tenth in one-over-par fives and then I birdied the par four eleventh hole with a three to go to two down. We halved the twelfth and thirteenth holes in par four and par five respectively. At this point I was still two down but at the short fourteenth he got in bunkers twice and a brave single putt only yielded a four. I got a three. So I was now one down. The fifteenth was a par five and he drove out of bounds. To his credit he used only four shots on his second ball to give him a six but I made five and the match was now all square. The sixteenth was quite a long par three, about 180 yards, and I hit my tee shot with a six iron dead straight but just short of the hole giving myself an uphill eight foot putt. He got a three but I sank the putt for a birdie two. For the first time in the match I was in the lead. I was one up with two holes to go. They were both par fours. We both got par fours at the seventeenth though he struggled to get up and down from just off the green. The same happened at the eighteenth where we both got par fours but where I was left with the last putt, a three footer for the match and the Club Championship. It fell in from the side and we shook hands. I still have the ball with the 'smile'. And I had the knowledge that from the back tees, the medal tees, I had played the second nine in 35 gross. It may well have been the best golf I have ever played and I had played it when it mattered. I was indeed the Club Champion, not so much in my estimation but rather in that of those who managed the Club's affairs. I was twenty two years old. I won various other competitions around this time at North Warwickshire, including the Final Medal in two consecutive years, including that same year, but no win mattered to me as much as the Radmore. It had been a test of nerve and skill.

Less than two years later, in 1966, I was to be in contention in the individual medal championship of the Solicitors' Golfing Society, The Law Society's National Championship. I do not know whether the solicitor's profession has a more than average share of good golfers compared with other occupations. I suspect it may have.

Anyway in the 1960s plenty of solicitors who were good golfers could make time to play. Control of your own time, as I well know from my own experience, enabled the self-employed professional man to catch up on a deliberate week day diversion at almost any other time of the day, night or weekend.

The solicitor-golfers assembled for their Annual Meeting and Championship in 1966 at Little Aston near Sutton Coldfield, not far from my home ground. The description 'millionaire golf', often overworked, is fully justified at Little Aston which is a magnificent golf course, membership carefully screened, maintained to the highest standards in the golfing world.

My start time in the individual championship of medal play over eighteen holes in the morning was 9.35 am and I hit a nice big drive off the first tee down the middle of the first fairway with a slow easy swing. As it happened I 'topped' my second shot with a nine iron on to the green (shades of the Radmore). But I got my par four. Then I settled down and

Chapter Nine – An Interlude On Golf

played some good golf until the twelfth hole, a par five, where I missed the fairway to the right and could not find my ball. If I think about it, this still puzzles me because I didn't miss the fairway by much and the rough was light. But I resigned myself to 'lost ball', went back to the tee and played another ball. I got that ball down in five strokes, result, with penalty, a seven. At the next hole, a par three, I put my seven iron approach close and holed the putt for a birdie two. The next hole, par four, I judged my drive just right, hit a nine iron to the flag and holed the putt again, for a birdie three. I held my game, just about, for the rest of the round and came out winner, I would be twenty four years old. You might say Golf Champion of my profession before I even had a practising certificate!

Checking the records of those years I find that I was a Radmore finalist in 1964 and 1966 and that I won the Final Medal in 1964 and 1965 including 79-10=69.

More curiously, I remember a 3-Club Competition played over nine holes at North Warwickshire Golf Club. We were allowed to chose which three clubs we would use. There was much talk at the Club among the members of using some other club in the bag to double-up as a putter. This would have involved setting out on the competition with three clubs none of which was a putter. This seemed to me like a recipe for "three putts" on every green. In other words three shots with a club ill-designed for the purpose rather than two (or less) with the proper tool. I kept my own counsel but I would have none of this. The putter I regarded as essential. It might be that Donald Carr could putt with a 3-iron or that, rather later, Ben Crenshaw could putt with a sand wedge hitting the ball half way up. I was not going to do it either way. Almost half my shots would be putts.

That decision was made. One of my three clubs would be a putter. Furthermore six of the nine holes would require the longest drive I could reasonably hit. There was no point in compromising over that, with only two other clubs in the bag, and the two long holes would need a wood for the second shot anyway if one was serious. That settled that the second club would be a 2-wood. For my third club I chose a 6-iron, a versatile club for full shots, half-shots and chipping and ideal for my tee shots at the two short holes.

This choice, and in particular the 6-iron, involved a gamble with bunkers if I got in to bunkers. I could play out of bunkers backwards with the 6-iron if I had to. In the event I didn't have to.

I had a clearly thought out strategy. With these three clubs I played the nine holes of the contest in thirty seven shots gross, one over par. I won by miles. I reflected that golf is a game of thinking about it.

Chapter 10

Practising The Law

"In my youth... I took to the law..."
(Advice from a caterpillar: Lewis Carroll)

When it was clear, a few weeks ahead of the event, that I was going to be admitted a solicitor in May 1966 and since, not unnaturally, that would mark an end to my articles of clerkship [1], I knew that I needed to think about what to do next. I had rather hoped that the firm with which I had served my articles, Reynolds & Co, and in particular my principal, Peter Root, would offer me an assistant solicitor's position with that firm. But they didn't. So I looked at the advertisements offering positions for young solicitors, not least in the Gazette of the Birmingham Law Society. There was, in particular, a rather challenging opportunity for a young solicitor ("could be a newly admitted man") to fill the gap created by the departure of a partner from a significant firm of solicitors in West Bromwich, called Lyon Clark & Co, who was going to open a new branch for that same firm in Wolverhampton. Whilst the man creating the vacancy at West Bromwich was a partner and would obviously remain so in Wolverhampton, with new challenges for him, it was clear that a significant challenge was also on offer for his replacement in West Bromwich and I went for it.

I was interviewed. The interview went well. It was soon clear they were going to offer me the job. They asked me how much money I wanted. The going rates for young solicitors at that time were between £800 and £1200 a year. So I asked for £1600 a year. There was a temporary look of shock by my interviewers. They asked me why I was out of line. I replied "because I am better than the others." There were no further questions. My appointment was agreed. My cockiness was back but this time it was based on some degree of self-belief.

Back at Reynolds & Co I sought a meeting with Peter Root, joined by Peter Perrey, the two partners who had had most to do with my period there in articles and told them that I wished to discuss with them what I was going to do next. They were solicitous and stood ready to give me their best advice.

I explained that I had been to see Lyon Clark & Co . They nodded and listened to what I had to say. I told them that I had been offered £1600 a year to work for that firm as an assistant solicitor. Whilst it was only

---

1. *The name then given to a trainee solicitor's apprenticeship.*

Chapter Ten – Practising The Law

betrayed for an instant, I noted their surprise. Then one of them, with the genuine seriousness of an older man to a younger man and, I have no doubt, wishing me well, said that it was a good offer and that I should accept it.

My time at Lyon Clark & Co was interesting in that it introduced me to advocacy before Magistrates and the County Court, to some splendid working colleagues, to West Bromwich Albion and to the Black Country. Although I did not know it at the time, of course, this was actually going to help me in Dudley in the future.

I worked hard and did well by Lyon Clark & Co. I started with a small caseload but built it up very rapidly. I kept a note of the bills, which I delivered for them representing profit costs to the firm. It was not long before, in a single month, I was delivering bills equal to the annual salary they were paying me. By whatever test, I was profitable to my employers. And so it was that at the end of my first year with Lyon Clark & Co I asked if my salary could be reviewed. They suggested an uplift of £100. I was very disappointed. I felt that if that was their response to my energy and enterprise then maybe my future did not lie with Lyon Clark & Co.

But then something quite unexpected happened. I was approached by Peter Root. Would I come back to Reynolds & Co as a salaried partner, with my name on the notepaper, to earn £2250 a year? I was delighted and accepted immediately. It swept away all the lingering disappointment about not having been offered a job by them when I first qualified. Then a thought occurred to me, a salutary corrective to my earlier attitude, that maybe Peter Root and Peter Perrey had played this more subtly than I thought. Perhaps they had thought, at the end of my articles, that I was indeed promotion material but that it would be a good idea to let me find my own way somewhere else for a time. I never tested this thought. I kept it to myself.

But I was anxious to deal properly with Lyon Clark & Co and I gave them three months notice and worked that three months notice assiduously. I indicated to them at the end that I would be taking four clients with me. They were evidently satisfied that the four clients in question were indeed mine rather than theirs, as it were, but I issued bills to each of the four clients in Lyon Clark's name so that Lyon Clark & Co was paid up to date for all the work I had done for these clients up to the time of my departure. I left Lyon Clark & Co on good terms with them which was important to me. My diligent and agreeable secretary, Irene Freeth came with me to Reynolds & Co to be my secretary in that new environment. I attended her wedding not long afterwards.

I had, incidentally, acquired an interesting new client during my time at West Bromwich. He was to become a very important and a very personal client. His name was Corrado Berghelli.

I met Corrado Berghelli for the first time in West Bromwich in the summer of 1966. He had been rather passed round the middle-ranking staff of Lyon Clark & Co, as a client, because most people could not understand his limited English. I have always had an ear for meaning rather than words and I could understand him and I found him rather interesting. He had arrived in England from Naples on a cargo ship mainly because the parents of the woman he wanted to marry would not allow this marriage because he was below their station. Happily she was to follow him and they married in England. In West Bromwich at that time there was an extensive compulsory purchase scheme for older properties which might have been described as slums. He lived at 14 Old Meeting Street, West Bromwich. It was such a property. At this stage I had a serious learning experience. My Solicitor's Finals Examinations had taught me nothing about the terms upon which Local Authorities could compulsorily acquire residential property nor about the critical test about fitness or unfitness for human habitation which very considerably affected the compensation which was to be paid to the compulsorily dispossessed.

I studied this and learned it quickly enough and got a good result for Corrado Berghelli and also acted for him and his wife in a parallel purchase of a rather nicer property at 57 Hill Top, West Bromwich. He was well and truly my client by now. He had a day job and a night job. By day he worked at the Accles & Pollock foundry and by night he worked at the Rainbow Casino as a croupier. He was earning and building up money as fast as he could. Within a few months he staggered into my office one morning, obviously depleted of sleep, wearing dark glasses and with a very significant amount of cash. He told me – this is my interpretation of what he said – that he was going to buy a lorry drivers' café in Solihull. It was known as 1097 Stratford Road, Monkspath, Shirley. I acted for him in this transaction and it went through successfully. I was well aware of this location and began to visit it. At first it consisted of a shop at the front selling crisps and lemonade and cigarettes and a rectangular room at the back with an adjacent kitchen. It was, for all practical purposes, a typical "greasy-spoon" pull-in. Pretty soon the beans on toast changed to spaghetti on toast and then in a relative whirlwind of transactions he bought the semi-detached property next door, number 1095, which had been residential, and knocked the two into one. Then he sold 57 Hill Top, West Bromwich and bought a residential property close by on the Stratford Road namely 997

Chapter Ten – Practising The Law

Stratford Road and moved close to his nascent Italian Restaurant. The next task was crucial which was to get him a "table licence" enabling him to sell wines and spirits in the café which, by this time, must properly be called a restaurant. This was difficult. In those days, this was the summer of 1966, the trading community which had the right to sell liquor whether by "on licence", "off licence" or "table licence" opposed all new entrants to the trade. I appeared for him in a contested application before Solihull Licensing Justices. In giving evidence himself he was a good witness. In his broken English he chose to understand the questions that he wanted to understand and dealt with the others in a kind of engaging pathos. The Clerk to the Court, George Taylor, not wrongly, was impatient with the objectors. He also wanted to get away to a wedding reception where he was due to make a speech and propose a toast.

Most of the objections were ultimately shown to be contrived. One was based, for example, on traffic movements to and from the new business that is to say vehicles turning into it from the Stratford Road and away from it on to the Stratford Road. But in the nature of his business these would no longer be lorries and lorry drivers but private motor cars and private diners. The balance of this hazard was in favour of the application. Corrado and I won. It was a beautiful summer's day. We went back to the restaurant and drank chianti. Not long afterwards he bought another café on the other side of the road, slightly further south, and he called it Villa Bianca. He used it as an overflow for the gigantic success of the over subscribed Da Corrado restaurant which he had brought into being in the combined premises of the lorry drivers' pull-in and its semi-detached residential neighbour. The business was a stunning success. It is to this day. I have taken meals there for over thirty years. He is dead now. I attended his funeral. But he really did something. The hardworking runaway from Naples via West Bromwich, my client, had created a stylish, trend-setting and enduring business in Solihull which bore his name.

Meanwhile I was building my practice largely as an extension of my social life. I got clients from Hampton-in-Arden Cricket Club, the Fentham Club and the White Lion and the Engine Hotel all in Hampton and the North Warwickshire Golf Club.

I had been lecturing in law in the evenings to students from the Institute of Marketing and the Institute of Retail Management at what is now Aston University in Birmingham and at what was then the Lanchester College in Coventry. The money had been quite useful, learning by teaching had been invaluable (you can't explain it if you don't understand it) and this activity also yielded me some clients.

On my return to Reynolds & Co I went back to their office in Newhall Street where the notepaper now reflected two new partners. The other one was John Grice with whom I had been at Bromsgrove. We were in the cricket eleven together. He had done me the honour of asking me to be best man at his wedding, which was a happy occasion. At the time of which I speak there was rivalry between John and me but it was healthy and did not disturb our friendship.

John was to die tragically young of leukemia on 12 December 1980 at the age of 38. What a loss.

Events moved quite quickly after my return to Reynolds & Co. First of all the firm moved offices from Newhall Street to Rutland House in Edmund Street and I helped with this move. Nor had I been back at the firm for many months before a decision was taken to open a new branch office of Reynolds & Co in Solihull. The firm already had a branch in Halesowen. I think the availability of premises helped spark the idea because the development of Mell Square in Solihull by Norwich Union had just been completed and it was mostly let. But Norwich Union themselves had retained, for their own purposes, a single ground floor retail unit at 30 Drury Lane. Their continuing presence on the site had outlived its usefulness and they were looking for a professional tenant on the understanding that such a tenant would pass on promptly any lingering inquiries intended for them. This did not seem too onerous an obligation and in the event there were very few such inquiries.

I was asked if I would take charge of the Solihull office. This was a wonderful opportunity and I accepted it gratefully.

The strategy, with which I wholeheartedly agreed, was that in building this new Solihull branch of Reynolds & Co, the soft option should be rigorously avoided of re-directing to it existing clients of the Birmingham firm who merely happened to live in Solihull of which there were a fair number.

Nothing should be done to discourage them from continuing to place their business with Rutland House in Birmingham.

I started, almost literally, with a capable and agreeable secretary –cum-receptionist called Rae Wilson, a typewriter and me. On Day One we had only those clients which could genuinely be called my own. On that first day we had three items of post of which one was a bill and another was for the Norwich Union.

I built it up with all my energy and it was not long before it was doing quite well. This was in 1968. Within a year we needed larger premises. The staff, by then, had risen to four, soon to be five and we moved to 58a Poplar

Chapter Ten – Practising The Law

Road in two floors over the Cheltenham & Gloucester Building Society. This had been Pattisons cake shop and restaurant which my mother and I had traditionally attended after successive Eversfield prize-givings in Solihull Council House which was then on the other side of Poplar Road. In the first floor of the restaurant was a window seat which I had always wanted to sit in on those occasions and in adapting the building as my new office, I kept it. We developed that building as we continued to expand and we were soon eight members of staff and at about this time, providentially, and to my eternal thankfulness, I recruited Mavis Ferguson who was to be my secretary for the next thirty years. Arguably she recruited me. By now I was an equity partner in Reynolds & Co and was shortly to take on Martin Allsopp, a very young qualified solicitor from Walsall, who was himself to become a salaried partner in Reynolds & Co in due course. As we expanded another move had become necessary and we transferred the Solihull practice to two quite large floors over the NatWest Bank at No 2 High Street, Solihull. I remarked that I had, at last, become the proverbial High Street Solicitor.

These new premises were splendidly located, not that the others had not been, and we took them over, in fact, from Evershed & Tomkinson Solicitors, who, in turn, were on the move. I was asked, not unnaturally, by Evershed & Tomkinson to redirect any of their clients, unaware of their move, who continued to turn up at the same premises. They didn't want me poaching any of their clients. As if I would.

In 1977 the politics of Reynolds & Co started to go wrong. It was not really any individual's fault but anyone who has worked in a partnership will know that there has to be an innate balance, hard to describe, but you know when you've got it and you know when you haven't. It has to be a balance of ages, because succession is important, and of skills as well as personalities and contributions and profit sharing. If a single spoke comes out of the wheel it can destabilise. The spoke, if I can call him that, that came out was Peter Root himself the relatively young senior partner and intellectually the best lawyer in the practice. He was placed in an incredibly difficult position. His biggest client was probably the firm's most prestigious, Allied Breweries. They had been through a very large phase of expansion, taking in many other businesses.

The Trust Deed governing their Pension Fund had had to be re-written because of all these acquisitions. It was an awesome and towering task. It required deep and certain knowledge of company law and taxation law, not least.

Peter Root and a senior executive from Allied Breweries called Stanley Plant, of whom Peter Root thought highly, had done it by themselves. The end product of their labours was hard backed and about the size of a volume of the Encyclopedia Britannica. It was a great achievement for any lawyer and most of us probably could not have attempted it.

Allied Breweries had come to account for almost all Peter Root's professional working time. Then came the bombshell. They announced that they were going to set up their own in-house legal team. There would be no more work for Reynolds & Co from Allied Breweries. The best and biggest client was going.

However they gave Peter Root first refusal on running this in-house legal department down in Bristol.

He was in an almost impossible position in that he really had no option. He was past his fiftieth birthday. He could try to rebuild his practice. He was certainly good enough to do that.

But he could take the secure salary and the pension that would follow. To no-one's surprise and with everyone's good wishes he chose to go to Allied Breweries.

I entered into discussions with Peter Perrey to see if we could devise a formula for the future of the firm of Reynolds & Co as it would be without Allied Breweries but, more especially, without Peter Root.

Both Perrey and I had enjoyed being partners of Root who had been the undisputed captain of the ship. How were we to get on when that captain went?

Perrey's real affection was for the Halesowen branch of Reynolds & Co, which he had started, whilst I was deeply committed to the Solihull branch of Reynolds & Co which I had started and which now employed eleven people. I asked Peter Perrey for parity between us in the partnership if we were effectively to go on running it together. Peter did not want this. I think he felt that he was entitled now to be senior partner. I do not blame him in the slightest. But so it was that I offered to buy the Solihull practice off Reynolds & Co. The negotiations were not that difficult. We made a calculation that my capital tied up in the firm as a whole was about equal to the value of the Solihull practice so I abandoned my capital position on paper and took the Solihull practice instead. I took Martin Allsopp into partnership and re-named the Solihull business Taylor Allsopp & Co.

I had an enormous admiration for Martin's ability (he was subsequently to become my own solicitor for certain transactions) but our ways were different and I think Taylor Allsopp & Co was always destined to spawn John Taylor & Co on the one hand and Allsopp & Co on the other which, in due course, it did. Meanwhile it was a temporarily convenient coalition of two men with different objectives.

Chapter Ten – Practising The Law

Looking back on that passage of events there is now a certain inevitability about them. I felt I had to get the Solihull practice out of Reynolds & Co, Martin was the obvious person to help me run it. Martin was ever likely to fly the nest himself one day as, in a sense, I had done.

Thereafter John Taylor & Co remained at 2 High Street and prospered. It would have prospered more if politics was not by now claiming a lot of my time. Then in 1985 the National Westminster Bank served notice on us that they wanted the first and second floors of 2 High Street back for their own use. And so we moved again, this time to Norwich House in Poplar Road, almost opposite where we had been at 58a over the Cheltenham & Gloucester Building Society. I was over a building society again, this time the Halifax. They were splendid premises, rather larger than we needed. I took a twenty five year lease and had a grand opening reception.

This was to prove to be a very good move indeed because in July 1988 I was invited to join the Government as a Whip. As I may have said elsewhere, in Government, Whips are Ministers and paid accordingly. Unsurprisingly I was sent a booklet from the Cabinet Office called Questions of Procedure for Ministers. It spoke in restrained language about the dangers of conflicts of interest. Despite the restrained language it was pretty vivid to me, and when I had finished reading it, the idea which had been forming in my mind for a while became fixed. It was time to sell the practice. This is where the twenty five year lease came in. Taken together with the steady performance of my firm, the goodwill of its clients and the value of work in progress, the lease gave me a package that I could sell. My staff were good too and whilst they would not be obliged to stay on under a new proprietor, I was going to make sure that their jobs would be secure under a new proprietor if I made a successful sale and if they wanted to stay.

The deal proved remarkably easy and trouble-free. I rang Peter Taylor (no relation), a former President of the Birmingham Law Society. He was then sole proprietor of Roland Evans & Taylor in Solihull. I reminded him of a chance pleasantry which we had once shared to the effect that if we merged our firms it would be a simple matter to predict a name for the merged practice. We would call it 'Taylors'.

And so we did.

Our practices were actually very complementary and their merger was convenient and mutual. Mine was strong on conveyancing and litigation. His was strong on company work and trusts and probate.

As soon as I telephoned him and recalled the conversation about the name of a merged practice he knew that I was serious and I was pleased

Please Stay To The Adjournment

to note that he was too. He invited me to go round and see him. I had written down nine suggested heads of agreement in handwriting on a single side of paper. I took it to him and I mentioned a purchase price that was consistent with the earnings record of my firm. It was a fair asking price. I did not ask too much. We rapidly reached agreement, decided that we did not need accountants or outside legal advice, and that we would tell no one, except our secretaries, and meet again the following day for a cup of coffee and, if we both still felt happy about it, a handshake. That is exactly what happened. Whereas I might normally have been in the weaker bargaining position, since I needed to get out, he was badly cramped in unsatisfactory offices and reckoned, rightly, that he could combine the staff of both our firms in the floor space which I had so recently secured.

Meanwhile I did indeed secure the jobs all my staff. He got the value of my business and clients. I worked hard to ensure they would stay. He got the premises he needed. I got my money, all installments paid on time.

The deal itself was concluded in a matter of days, no more than a week. I had always observed that one of the hardest things in business was knowing when and how to sell it. It was a matter of some satisfaction that I had met the test myself.

I spent my last morning in Court pleading a case before Solihull Magistrates. Naturally I did not indulge myself by telling them that it was the last time I would appear before them as an advocate. The morning belonged to the client and I was there to do my best for him and not for some kind of valedictory flourish. Only later did the Magistrates find out that it had indeed been my last case before them whereupon they sent me a very nice letter concerning the many years I had practiced before them in Solihull.

It was a glorious late morning when I left the Magistrates Court that day for the last time as an advocate. I wondered if I would feel emotional or nostalgic. After all I had practised as a solicitor from 1966 to 1988. In fact I felt happy, uplifted almost. I thought I had done a pretty good job over those years and I had left on my own terms and with a modestly developing political career ahead of me.

My relationship with Peter Perrey remains sound and stimulating. He proposed my health superbly well at both my 50th and 60th birthdays. Regarding friendships his advice remains: "Grapple them to thy soul with loops of steel." [1]

Three younger men I may have helped in their legal careers: Stephen Karle, Paul Gilks and Paul Saunders all came to my firm initially as

---

1. Hamlet: Polonius to Laertes.

Chapter Ten – Practising The Law

students for work experience. All went on to do extremely well, as lawyers and other things too. They are my protegees. I rejoice in their success and wish them fulfilment.

Even a cursory retrospection on my career as a solicitor would be incomplete without reference to one other very remarkable client and friend.

Malcolm King was capable of anything and proved it. He came to me as my client many years ago by delegation from Peter Root. We recommended him, for Chartered Accountancy services, to Leonard (Len) Wilson, himself a great friend to Peter and me from Hampton-in-Arden Cricket Club. Malcolm and Len worked very well together and the relationship prospered.

Malcolm was, and is, a brilliant and successful adventurer and entrepreneur beyond any other known to me.[2] He remains so. I have endeavoured to keep in touch with him. If you read this Malcolm I wish you "happy hunting".

Post Script on the origins of the Solihull Duty Solicitor Scheme

In 1973/4 Denis Gray who was then the Chairman of the Solihull Magistrates Bench suggested to a meeting of those local solicitors who appeared regularly in Solihull Magistrates Court that we might care to consider setting up a Duty Solicitor Scheme. That is to say that we should establish a rota by reference to which one of us would be at Court every sitting morning to be available to any unrepresented defendant who found that he or she needed advice after all or even representation. It was by no means unusual for unrepresented defendants to arrive at Court thinking that they knew what to do but then running in to uncertainty. In such cases, whilst the Clerk to the Court would always try and be helpful, it was of course inherently unhealthy for the Clerk to the Court to trespass into the realms of being the defendant's adviser. Nor were the Magistrates comfortable about that, quite rightly. They were much more attracted by the prospect of being able to say to such a defendant "Why don't you go and have a word with the Duty Solicitor? Meanwhile we will put your case back for a short time."

In those days, whilst this embryonic concept of a Duty Solicitor was commendable (and it commended itself to me) it then represented very new thinking, avant garde even. It went against the grain of the Law Society's own rules of professional conduct which were quite heavily loaded in favour of the sanctity of the unfettered right of the defendant to choose his or her own adviser or representative.

---

2. One rival for this accolade, met by me much more recently, and as MP for Solihull rather than as a solicitor, might be Ted Tuppen of Enterprise Inns plc whose head office is now happily in Monkspath in my constituency.

In due course I was to become one of the three local solicitors who pioneered and introduced the Solihull Duty Solicitor Scheme. The other two were Iain Jollie and Edgar Seagroatt. In the course of this we travelled to the Law Society in Chancery Lane to make a formal application for a derogation from the Society's rules of professional conduct to permit the Scheme. We were aware that we were introducing a pilot or prototype and it was a fascinating piece of pioneering. These days Duty Solicitor Schemes are to be found in almost all Magistrates Courts, they are recognised in statute and funded by the Legal Aid Board.

Incidentally Denis Gray was not merely Chairman of the Solihull Bench and Chairman of the Solihull Magistrates Courts Committee but was a prominent Magistrate nationally. He was for some time Chairman of the Central Council of Magistrates Courts Committees and he devoted a lot of time working with the Home Office and in helping the Lord Chancellor's Department with the training of Magistrates. In this he was much assisted and encouraged, locally, by Solihull's excellent Clerk to the Justices, George Taylor.

Meanwhile, in the story of the Duty Solicitor Scheme, I think Denis Gray's ultimate hope may have been the setting up at some time in the future of a National Defender Scheme. I think he saw a Duty Solicitor Scheme as a step in the right direction. By contrast I saw it as a step complete in itself. The scheme would be run by the profession for the profession in addition to the more objective benefits that it would bring for the Magistrates, their Clerks and, in particular, those unrepresented defendants whose confidence that they knew their situation and how to handle it often melted on the day.

I look back with some pleasure on having played a part in the pioneering of a Duty Solicitor Scheme. It proved to be a successful and enduring one. It is not too much to claim that the Solihull initiative, taken forward mainly by Denis Gray and me, helped to lay the ground for a serious improvement in criminal justice at the point of entry to the system.

At about the same time, in 1973, by now a County Councillor, I was a formative influence in the initiative known as the Shirley Centre for Community Help. This spawned the Shirley C.A.B. which came to be an astonishing success story and is so to this day.

I initiated another campaign which was to have a County Court for Solihull. In this I did not succeed. Solihull, almost alone amongst Metropolitan Boroughs, does not possess its own County Court. Its users generally use Birmingham County Court although there is now more flexibility. Plaintiffs may choose their own court of origination but may find themselves deflected to the jurisdiction more convenient to a defendant.

Chapter 11

Beginnings Of Politics

How did I get into this?

In an earlier part of this story, I describe how, at the age of eighteen, I came to realise that I was more interested in politics than most of the other boys at school with me. Earlier than that there had been a teenage birthday party for Anne Taylor, no relation, though they lived opposite us in Meriden Road in Hampton-in-Arden. Her father Eric Taylor, very clumsily as I thought then, called an exuberant birthday party to order and went round the room asking us all what we wanted to do when we grew up. I have, to this day, three contemporary witnesses who would say that, when it was my turn, I said I wanted to be a Member of Parliament. For myself whilst, I do remember the birthday party, I must say that I do not remember this answer given by me. But I will not deny it and the evidence, from three pristine disinterested, sources, is pretty convincing.

My first foray into public elective politics was the Hampton-in-Arden Parish Council Elections of 1966. I would have been twenty four and working as an Assistant Solicitor with the firm of Lyon Clark & Co in West Bromwich. I remained a resident of my native village, though my parents had moved to Norfolk by then. I thought that it would be a political start for me. It was not to be. And I learned an important lesson. In the list of names, I think there were about 16 for about 8 places, alphabetical priority is important. All else being equal, Adams will beat Young. I seriously considered putting out a manifesto saying I would judge each issue on its merits and in the best interests of the village. A rather Conservative approach, looking back on it. If I had done so and distributed it adequately, I think I might have won. Anyway I didn't. That was the close of that modest campaign and in 1969 I moved to Solihull and into what was, at that time, a different electoral area.

To be precise, I moved to 19 Emscote Green, Solihull, joined the St Alphege branch of the Solihull Conservative Association and thought of trying to get elected to a more significant Local Authority. I had Birmingham City Council in mind. I considered, additionally, renting a flat in Bantry Close in Sheldon which was both in Birmingham and as near as possible to Solihull. My idea was to provide the foundation for election to Birmingham City Council which I regarded as major league local

Please Stay To The Adjournment

government, as indeed it was. But I was discouraged in this by Ivor Freeman, Chief Conservative agent in Birmingham, with whom I went for an interview. He thought that there would be no harm in my sticking with local government prospects in Solihull itself.

The nature of local politics in Solihull in those days, as I may refer to again, can best be described as semi-independent. The Conservatives traditionally contested some seats but ceded others to candidates put up by the established and reputable Residents Associations which had become a feature of civic and community life in Solihull. Walter Langley, the Conservative agent in Solihull, was a master of this finesse and encouraged me to seek an independent nomination from one of these Residents Associations. Two vacancies were available at that time in the fiefdom of the St Alphege Residents Association and, as it turned out, when I applied there were three candidates for two places. One of them was Vincent Humberstone, a former Labour Councillor on Solihull Council. The other was a Mrs Howe. I was running with cold and had taken antihistamine. We were all interviewed. I lost. I was asked if I wished to stay for the rest of the meeting. I judged that the right thing was to hang on despite my disappointment. I said I wanted to and did but I believe, from time to time, the antihistamine taking its toll, I drifted off to sleep. This exercise can only be described as a complete failure.

I went back to Walter Langley. His next advice was that I should seek membership of the List of approved Conservative local government candidates in Solihull. I did so. I went before a small committee, chaired by Michael Haycock, asking for this approval. As a foretaste of future experiences, I was at first refused. I was asked to do some more work in the Party before being admitted to the List. I threw myself into the work of the St Alphege branch, with a membership recruiting brief, and also as Social Secretary. In these efforts I think I can say that I generated more money for the Party than the Branch Treasurer.

At the second time of asking I was admitted to the local list of approved Conservative council candidates.

Not long after, that good man Ron Foster, then a Conservative Councillor for Shirley South, ran into difficulties with his Draper's business and had to resign as a Councillor. There was a by-election in prospect.

Then all sorts of new things began to happen. Ron Foster had held that seat in the name of the Conservative Party. A selection procedure began to decide who would be the new Conservative candidate for the contest for Ron's vacated seat. The local Conservatives were certainly going to try to hold on to it.

Chapter Eleven – Beginnings Of Politics

I applied and was invited for interview. Here came the influence of Walter Langley. Looking back on it, he had already decided that I should be the candidate. A selection committee was set up chaired by the admirable Alderman Les Coombes. I suppose half a dozen people sat there at the committee of selection and I was asked various questions with which I had no difficulty. Then I was asked about my community involvements. There weren't many! Before I could answer, Walter Langley told the meeting that my community involvements were of a confidential, charitable nature connected with my law practise. He was pulling for me and I knew it. His intervention seemed to satisfy the selectors. With little further formality I got the nomination. I was now in a position to fight my first election as a Conservative candidate.

Chapter 12

Councillor

"The people get the elected representatives they deserve"

In 1954 I had taken a photograph of Princess Margaret in an open car as she passed Eversfield School on the Warwick Road. We were lined up on the pavement outside school for the purpose of watching her go by. The reason for her visit was the elevation of Solihull to the status of a Borough.

The Solihull Municipality had developed during the twentieth century, graduating from a Rural District Council to an Urban District Council in 1932 and to a Borough Council on the occasion which I have described.

Solihull went on to become a County Borough in 1964 and a Metropolitan Borough in 1974.

Local politics in Solihull in 1971 when I fought my by-election were unusual. The Conservative Association had long taken a view of its local purpose which was primarily to return a Conservative MP, secondarily to raise money for the Conservative Party and only thirdly to support and return Conservative Councillors in certain wards where that was thought to be appropriate.

Public commotion about the level of rates charged to its citizens by Solihull Council in the 1930s had spawned a Federation of vigilant Residents Associations which in 1971 were still active in certain wards. They put up their own Independent local candidates for the Council in those wards, and they invariably won, frequently unopposed. These Independents were not unusually paid-up members of the Conservative party. The Solihull Conservative Association chose to acquiesce in this process and only put up Conservative candidates in those wards where a Labour or Liberal candidate was otherwise thought likely to win.

Shirley South was such a ward. So, at the time of which I speak, I sought to become elected as a Conservative Councillor in a ward where a contest was normal. A Conservative candidacy was therefore normal too and I could certainly expect at least a Labour opponent who was, in the event, to be Edmond Stiles. On its own small scale, it was regular politics.

There was a small 'active' membership of the ward branch. They were elderly. Their goodwill to me and support for me were unquestioned and appreciated by me but I had to find the 'arms and legs' to deliver my election address leaflets, letter box by letter box, and, more demandingly,

Chapter Twelve – Councillor

to canvass from door to door to present my candidacy personally and seek pledges of support. I drew down heavily on my personal friends, not least from Hampton-in-Arden Cricket Club, for this purpose and I did so successfully. In the end we achieved something which I have never known elsewhere in any election that I have ever been involved in, that is to say a 100% canvass.

At all times I was greatly helped by Alderman Coombes who was undeniably and worthily the dominant local political figure in the area. At one stage he drove me round the ward boundaries fully to acquaint me with the ground that I was contesting. There was a meeting of the Council that occurred during the three weeks of the election campaign. He secured me a place in the gallery so that I could witness that occasion and pick up whatever was relevant in terms of debated local issues.

But the real canvassing was done by me. For three weeks I went out three hours a night between 6.00pm and 9.00pm.

Polling day and the count were on Thursday 21 October 1971, Trafalgar Day. It had been a huge effort. I won by almost 2:1 (1161 votes against 676 votes to my opponent) and was declared elected Councillor for the Shirley South ward. Any number of Conservative Councillors came to my count to see me elected who had not worked for me at all.

The following morning I went to see the Town Clerk, Denys Chapman, who administered my Declaration of Office, gave me my copy of the Council Year Book, agendas and minutes, and other documents relevant to the working of the Council. I took these to The George Hotel where I treated myself to a celebratory lunch.

Just over three weeks later on Sunday 14 November 1971, dressed in the tricorn hat and gown of a Councillor, I processed with the rest of the Council from the Council House to the War Memorial and the Parish Church for Armistice Sunday, my first formal civic duty.

The beginnings of politics in my terms was over. I was a Councillor. I had an elected mandate from the people of Solihull that was to be unbroken in one form or another until the present time. This was 1971. I was 30 years old.

Having become a Councillor enabled me to join a number of 'outside bodies' on which the Council enjoyed representation. That was to give me the community involvements which I had not possessed at the time of the selection meeting, such as school governorships, membership of youth club management committees, an interest in the Citizens Advice Bureau and all the rest. I had begun the development of a serious political C.V.

Chapter 13

The West Midlands County Council - Part 1

"This great County": Sir Francis Griffin (Did he mean it?)

When Edward Heath became Prime Minister in June 1970 he made Peter Walker Secretary of State for his newly created and far-reaching Department of the Environment. Peter Walker is a man I have always admired. Much later I came to work with him. He was Secretary of State for Wales from June 1987-May 1990. I was the government's Welsh Whip in the House of Commons from July 1988-April 1992.

His proposals for the reform of Local Government, ultimately enshrined in the Local Government Act of 1972, were radical, controversial and in some areas bitterly opposed. The main thrust, for the purposes of this account, was the creation of six provincial Metropolitan County Councils which came to be known as Greater Manchester, Merseyside, South Yorkshire, West Yorkshire, Tyne & Wear and West Midlands. Taking these in order, the big Cities that lay in the heart of each of these conurbations were Manchester, Liverpool, Sheffield, Leeds, Newcastle and Birmingham.

The largest of these was West Midlands Metropolitan County with a population of almost three million people. It was to be the second largest Local Authority in England after the Greater London Council (GLC).

The seeds of dissension lay in the fact that this was to be two-tier Local Government with each Metropolitan County made up of a series of Metropolitan Districts. Taking the case of the West Midlands, it was to comprise seven Metropolitan Districts: the Cities of Birmingham and Coventry and the Boroughs of Dudley, Sandwell, Solihull, Walsall and Wolverhampton (now more recently a City). The County Borough of Stourbridge was swept into Dudley, against its instincts, likewise the Urban District of Aldridge & Brownhills into Walsall. Meanwhile Sandwell was a new entity uneasily combining the County Boroughs of Warley and West Bromwich. Warley, it should be noted, having itself only relatively recently been formed as a merger of Smethwick and Oldbury. What a recipe!

There were two principal causes of bitterness.

First, most of these newly designated "Metropolitan Districts" in the course of their recent past or even, in many cases, their long term past had not been subordinated to anything called a County. They had been unitary authorities. It would have been true to say that Birmingham City Council,

Chapter Thirteen – The West Midlands County Council - Part 1

its leadership and its Lord Mayoralty had not considered anything politically superior to themselves whatever, except perhaps the Cabinet, and they would have thought twice about that!

The second cause of bitterness was the rivalry between the seven component Metropolitan Districts. It was hard to get Wolverhampton Councillors to speak to Birmingham Councillors, as I was to find out. Birmingham was Big Brother, disliked by the other authorities and inclined to throw its weight about. Expansionist desires had never been out of Birmingham's mind. Birmingham's reach-out developments into Chelmsley Wood, in Meriden and Frankley, in Bromsgrove were cases in point. Birmingham's absorption of the Royal Borough of Sutton Coldfield is still rancorously resented, in Sutton Coldfield. It is, I think, by ironic contrast, resented by Birmingham that the National Exhibition Centre and Birmingham Airport are in Solihull, subject to my Borough's planning controls, and not in Birmingham.

In due course the new Metropolitan County, its Council yet to be elected, was partitioned for that purpose into electoral *divisions*. (Contrast the naming of the electoral parts of District Councils or Borough Councils, which are called *wards*.) There were to be 104 County *divisions*, each to return one County Councillor.

The 17 *wards* of Solihull Borough Council were to be variously amalgamated to form 7 of these 104 County *divisions*. One of the seven Solihull *divisions* was a combination of the Shirley East, Shirley South and Shirley West *wards* of Solihull Borough Council and it was to be called simply, and appropriately, the Shirley *division*. I was, of course, already a Borough Councillor representing Shirley South *ward* and prospective parliamentary candidate for Dudley East, as will be seen in the next Chapter. It made sense for me to seek the Conservative nomination for the Shirley *division* of the County Council because it could be presented as a link between my Local Government base, in Solihull, and my parliamentary attempt in Dudley, both being in the same new County of West Midlands. I got the Conservative nomination for Shirley and I got elected, easily.

But we were hammered in the overall return. When the results were in on 12th April 1973, the Labour Party got 73 seats on this new Metropolitan County Council, we got 27 and the Liberals (as they were then still called) got 4.

The newly elected 27 Conservative County Councillors met at the Birmingham Conservative Club in the immediate aftermath of the result.

We had to choose a leader. There did not seem to be much doubt about the outcome. Sir Francis Griffin, a great former leader of Birmingham's City

"Ten blokes to give us a hundred ?"

"Yes, and I've thought about who the ten blokes might be and I've written them down here."

"Can I see that list?"

"Here it is."

"Well I see."

"Now what I suggest is that you and I take our John round to see each of these and John can say a few words about what the Election is about then we'll allow the man on the list ...."

"The man we've taken John to see?"

"Yes, the man on the list that we've taken John to see will be allowed to ask John a question and John will answer it."

"What then?"

"We'll ask him for a hundred pounds towards John's election campaign expenses."

"What a good idea."

"I thought you'd like it."

We then went round each of the ten. At the first, with the intended donor facing me and Luing and George sitting either side of him, I said my few words about what I thought were the important issues in the election. The intended donor proceeded to ask me a question. I answered it to the best of my ability. The intended donor appeared satisfied and, with solicitous encouragement from my two minders, reached into an inside pocket of his jacket and produced a cheque book. My minders smiled at him approvingly. He wrote out a cheque for a hundred pounds. Thanks, good wishes and handshakes were exchanged. My minders moved me on.

The same thing happened on the second occasion and the third and indeed on all subsequent occasions up to and including the ninth.

Then we went to the tenth.

This was to see Herman Smith of Herman Smith Ltd, a Dudley foundry and engineering group originated by his father of the same name at the turn of the century.

The atmosphere of the business certainly seemed established, dynastic even, as we entered the fine oak panelled board room hung with portraits, including, naturally enough, one of my host's father. The board table was very long. The current Herman Smith sat at one end and I sat a very long way from him at the other. My minders were either side of him. The set-piece was enacted. The previous pattern was followed. But Herman Smith started to ask a second question.

Chapter Fourteen – An Interlude On Dudley East

At this, George Griffiths interrupted him. "Herman, if you want to ask a second question it'll cost you two hundred pounds". All three men rocked with laughter considering that was very funny, which it was.

Herman Smith paid a hundred pounds like all the others.

As I look back on it, but I had an inkling of it then, this had been contrived, fixed and prepared in an orderly way. It was stage-managed. George Griffiths and Luing Preedy had agreed what conversation they would hold in front of me. They had agreed the visits to the donors. They had well primed the donors who knew what was expected of them. They had agreed. In one sense it was a charade. But in many ways a very important charade. Luing Preedy and George Griffiths knew that it would cost money to fight an election campaign. They wanted me to know that and they wanted me to play a part in the raising of the money. It was humbling, informative and incredibly well done. They could have raised that money from those sources anyway. They wanted me to be involved in it. They wanted me to understand. They wanted me to know that elections, on the ground, could not be fought without money and that the candidate must never take the fund raising for granted.

I well remember at the outset of that first campaign, asking for the canvass cards for the good areas and being quite impressed by the results. Then, after about three extended and intensive outings canvassing of the door steps asking my agent, Joyce MacDonald, for some more cards for the good areas and being told "there aren't any other good areas".

In the second General Election of 1974, in Dudley East, I had indicated that I would be prepared to stand again in the same seat.

This was well received. I knew that it was the right thing for me to do. I was not going to get a winning seat. The best thing for me, and I hope for them, was that I would 'stand by my bed' and fight Dudley East again.

This time we had another, different, entertaining moment.

Under the stairs of the Dudley Conservative Club we found we had a second set of loud speaker equipment. Now I had hired a campaign vehicle, a Land Rover, to which the first set of loud speaker equipment, the only one I thought we had, was already fitted. Now we had another.

There was an informal meeting at Dudley Conservative Club during a Saturday lunchtime to decide how we might use these new unexpected riches, the second set of loud speaker equipment.

Councillor Bob Griffiths, no relation to Alderman George Griffiths, suggested that I could use his car on which to mount the second set. Careful of the damage that it might do to the body work of his car to crimp on the loud speakers I gently asked my volunteer how he thought I might fix the speakers to his car.

"John, as far as I am concerned, you can nail 'em on."

The wonderful humour of these people was only part of their tremendous quality. I knew I couldn't win and they knew I couldn't win but it did not stop them. Twice in one year, they gave me three weeks of their time to fight two campaigns which never admitted defeat until after the declaration at each of the two counts and only then with heads held high. In the February election I was comfortably beaten in a two way fight with Labour and in the October election I was again comfortably defeated but this time in a four way contest with a Liberal candidate and a National Front candidate joining in as well.

My first count was memorable for a number of reasons. It was, as I have said, a two way fight. My successful Labour opponent was John (now Lord) Gilbert. Election night had seen torrential rain and my team and I had worked right up to the close of poll at ten o'clock. I had been soaked. John Gilbert, a good looking man anyway, looked immaculate in an expensive suit and with his wife and two attractive daughters. If it had not been for the rosettes it would have been confusingly difficult to "spot the Tory". Incidentally, I was the first Conservative candidate ever to fight Dudley in blue. Historically the Conservative party had contested that part of the world in red, white and blue or even in red! The winner spoke first and addressed the very large number of people who had assembled for the declaration in Dudley Town Hall. It was easy to see that we were hugely out-numbered. Gilbert went to the microphone first and commenced his address "Comrades...". I have never heard the word articulated in such a plummy way. It was a curious piece of incongruity. When it was my turn, I thanked all concerned, especially my own supporters, and said that I realised that there were no prizes for coming second but that I would return to Dudley and fight it again.

As I stepped down off the platform and into the hall any number of burly Labour supporters took my hand and said "well done lad" and they meant it. It was the inherent decency of these people. They knew that I hadn't a hope but that I had tried.

The broader memory of that night is that it was to be the defeat of the Heath Government. It took about forty eight hours for this to become quite clear whereupon Joe Rowley, then Chairman of the Dudley East Conservative Association, told me how grave he thought it all was and that I should address a general meeting of the Association to give them my views on what it all meant.

It had been the Election concerning the miners, the three day week, "who governs Britain?", Joe Gormley, Midland Bank profits, Arthur Scargill, Campbell Adamson, the battle of Saltley Gasworks et al.

Chapter Fourteen – An Interlude On Dudley East

The main assembly hall of Dudley Grammar School was hired for the purpose. I no longer remember all that I said but it seemed to be received seriously and well.

I ended by saying that it was not merely a defeat but that the battle would at some future time have to be fought all over again and won. Eleven years later, under Margaret Thatcher, it was.

Incidentally, many still believe that if the election of February 1974 had been held three weeks earlier that is to say on February 7 rather than on February 28, the Conservatives would have won.

Harold Wilson consolidated his extremely slender majority in the October election of that year.

It was a year that ended for me with two parliamentary contests on my CV, enormous gratitude to those who had helped me, a great respect for the people of Dudley, a fund of wonderful stories and an enduring readiness to go back there whenever I am asked.

Chapter 15

The West Midlands County Council - Part 2

(How I became a prisoner in six mile triangle)

In 1975, when we were still in opposition, half way through a Labour controlled four-year term, Sir Francis Griffin announced his retirement from the leadership of the Conservative Group on the West Midlands County Council.

Anthony Beaumont-Dark from Birmingham (now Sir Anthony) got himself nominated to succeed as Leader so did Peter Farmer from Wolverhampton and David Gilroy Bevan also from Birmingham and I, from Solihull, did too.

I entered the contest initially to combat the "juniority" with which I found myself saddled. It was at first a candidacy of protest. But then things started to change. At the Spring Meeting of the West Midlands Conservative Area Conference, at Llandrindod Wells, Councillor Bert Smith, boss (American style) of the Walsall Conservatives and Councillor Gilbert Richards, likewise of the Coventry Conservatives, told me not just that my candidature was realistic but that they thought I could win. Furthermore they said they would work for me. Naturally, I accepted gratefully. Decisions were then made as to which of the three of us would contact each of the other members of the Conservative County Council Group which was, for this purpose, the electorate.

I won the contest on the third ballot of an exhaustive eliminator. This is an election method to deal with a contest between several candidates for one place in which bottom placed candidates are eliminated after each successive ballot until one candidate emerges with an overall majority whereupon that candidate is declared the winner. This is an election method which I have always thought fair and commendable. I am left in no doubt that the reason I won was that I was the non-Birmingham candidate.

I then addressed the question of how to be the Leader, of the Opposition, on a very large Authority with disparate interests. The most important thing of all, of course, was how to win control of that Authority. Without that we would not be in a position to bring about change. Its' next election was to be on 5 May 1977 when all its 104 single-member seats would be vacated for contest.

Chapter Fifteen – The West Midlands County Council - Part 2

I asked all of my Opposition Spokesmen, whom I renamed Shadow Chairmen as of the various committees to produce for me in writing what they would like us to do in office. Over time we discussed and agreed final versions which ultimately graduated into our Manifesto. Thanks, not least, to Alan Hope, our Councillor for Birmingham (Perry Barr), who owned a printing firm, we produced this document impressively (if not quite to the standard of Millbank 1997) and also in several languages to try to connect with the significant immigrant populations in the West Midlands County.

I addressed the new group of Conservative candidates for the pending election. I roused them in the terms of Scipio Africanus towards the end of the third and decisive Punic War, when he laid siege to Carthage, and commanded his army to leave no masonry standing and nothing living alive. That that should be their purpose in this election. It was a bit hot for some. Others rather liked it.

Then we won everything that we could possibly have expected to win. As I waited for my own result in Solihull, I telephoned the Chief Executive of the County Council to learn from him what results were already in. He told me that a certain Bill Harris (Bill was already a friend of mine through my Dudley Parliamentary contests in 1974) had been declared the winner in Netherton and Woodside in Dudley and that there was a re-count in Chelmsley Wood. From my knowledge of the Dudley East constituency I was in not the slightest doubt that Netherton and Woodside could only be won by a Conservative candidate in a very favourable election. Chelmsley Wood, in northern Solihull and in a completely different part of the County, was overwhelmingly Labour. A re-count in Chelmsley Wood, whatever the final outcome, told its own story. Soon after I was to win Shirley with a majority which would have been comfortable in a Parliamentary Constituency, never mind a County Division. By this time I knew the night was ours.

We won 81 seats (up from 27), Labour won 19 (down from 73) and the Liberals again won 4.

On the morning of Friday 6 May 1977 I mounted the steps of County Hall. I was Leader of the County Council.

One of the first things we did was to reduce a vast and incoherent committee structure left behind by Labour. By now they had managed the inglorious achievement of over one hundred committees, sub-committees and working parties. I had designed a new committee structure during the election (outside the campaign but ready for winning) comprising eleven principal committees namely:-

Policy & Priorities,
Airports,
Finance,
Fire Services,
Highways,
Legal & Property,
Personnel & Administration,
Planning,
Police,
Transport, and
Waste Disposal & Pollution Control.

Additionally there were to be two sub-committees, one to be called Employment Commerce & Industry which was to report to the Policy Committee. The other was to be called Trading Standards which was to report to the Legal and Property Committee. The reduction of these two subject areas to sub committee status was deliberate and attracted attention. We were criticised, or rather I was, for down-grading the role of the County Council both as an Economic Planner and as an instrument of Consumer Protection. The critics were right in their interpretation of our actions. The truth of the matter was that the County Council had no statutory competence in economic planning which had been a great pretension of the previous administration and we were quite happy to lay that bare.

Likewise Labour had been excessive and zealous in Consumer Protection to the point, we thought, of making life tough for small traders whom they had already enraged by embarking upon a very Socialist set of Municipal Trading proposals. They had threatened to compete with their own business ratepayers! A reining-in of these activities was a signal that we were very happy to give and the change of the name from Consumer Protection to Trading Standards was also an indication of our intention to be even-handed between the consumer and the trader.

I took the Chair of the Policy & Priorities Committee and served on no other. I got my desired appointees made Chairmen of the other principal Committees and made them, as such, members of the Policy & Priorities Committee as well. All the principal Committees were to have sixteen members, quite enough, to include appropriate representation for the opposition parties.

The exception to this was the Policy & Priorities Committee, chaired by me, which was to be exclusively of my party. Twelve, I recommended, were

Chapter Fifteen – The West Midlands County Council - Part 2

to be chosen by me. They were the chairmen of all the other principal committees, who were my appointees anyway. The other four places I gave to the Conservative Group to elect. I also proposed that the same persons who were members of the Policy Committee should constitute the Group Executive. Otherwise I could foresee rivalry between the Policy Committee and the Group Executive and my having to fight various battles from time to time twice over. This was a lesson learned from observation of the Labour Party. Both in Government and in opposition, Labour leaders had had to struggle with getting policies though either a Shadow Cabinet or a Cabinet as well as through the Labour Party's National Executive.

I had some critics of this authoritarianism but I got my way. There were going to be real difficulties and agonising (for me) problems ahead. This was no time to compromise the authority which I had won.

We put our manifesto into effect very rapidly indeed and had the pleasure of producing a Statement of Achievement after exactly One Hundred Days. This was a self-indulgent simulation of the early days of President Kennedy's administration.

There was unease at first amongst the Officers of the County Council not least over our declared intention substantially to raise the bus fares. We were warned that there would be a terrible loss of "ridership". In the event there was no measurable loss of ridership at all. I think people realised time was up for Labour's previous frozen fares policy.

The most competent of all the officers was Derryck Hender, the Chief Executive. My inner circle and I had thought that he had been too closely associated with the policies of the previous administration. In the end he was to provide us with a refreshing surprise. Within hours of our winning control I had a conversation with him in which he said "Councillor Taylor, I have built council houses for Labour Authorities and sold them for Conservative Authorities; I have built up direct work labour units for Labour Authorities and run them down for Conservative Authorities. I am here to help you with your policies".

Well that was good. The next thing he said was perhaps even more surprising. We had intended to close down the proliferation of "Shoppers Shops" which Labour had introduced as a kind of consumer protection gone mad. "Grown men running up and down the High Street trying to find the cheapest pork chop" as Anthony Beaumont-Dark brutally, and effectively, stigmatised the scheme.

Derryck Hender looked at me and said "Councillor Taylor, I must warn you about your policy of promising to close all the Shoppers Shops by the end of the year". This was May. All of a sudden I had a sinking feeling that he was about to reverse his commitment of a moment before to help us carry out our policies. I asked him what he meant. He replied that closing the Shoppers Shops by the end of the year would cause real trouble and that we would be far better advised to close them by the end of the month!

I began to get on well with Derryck Hender and I think we strengthened our relationship by adopting a rather old fashioned convention that I would always call him Mr Hender and he would call me Councillor Taylor. In later years, when we were not in the position of Leader and Chief Executive we dropped the convention in favour of Christian names. But I do not think that it was a bad idea at the time to keep ourselves at somewhere near arms length and with a mutual respect for the fact that we had different roles. A distinction that is sometimes lost sight of in Local Government and never, in my opinion, with any good result from it.

Relations with the seven District Councils were not easy but I had long decided that we would, from the outset, abandon the previous Administration's practice of trying to meet them collectively in a sort of Grand Committee. The very idea had been doomed, I felt, and every such meeting had produced complex, seething, hostile alliances.

I made it my business to strike up one-to-one relationships with the leaders of the seven District Authorities. It did not work badly at all. But it could never have avoided two turbulent winters when the County Council, as Highway Authority, and Birmingham Council as the County's Highway agent, fumed and snarled at each other over the preferred procedures for providing winter gritting of the roads. It is a salutary lesson in politics that the bitterest battles can be about things that the general citizen would regard as absurd and not worth the trouble. Anyway the battles of Winter Gritting in our first two winters were, to that point, my toughest experience in politics. We finally put an end to them by ending District Agencies and doing the work directly as Highway Authority. They were really symbolic of the power struggle that existed between the West Midlands County Council and the Birmingham City Council not least, or even especially, at officer level. The actual dispute could have been about anything. It was a row waiting to happen.

Never having encountered anything quite like that before, I asked Derryck Hender if it was unusual in Local Government or whether there were often clashes between different Authorities. A native of Great Yarmouth, he told me that in Norfolk there had often been battles between Norfolk County Council on the one hand and Norwich City Council on the other. I asked him how long this had been going on. "Oh", he said, "about a thousand years."

Chapter Fifteen – The West Midlands County Council - Part 2

My personal commitment, as Leader, to running the County Council was enormous. In addition to managing my law practice, which was at that time immensely demanding, the additional responsibility for the County Council committed me, not unwillingly, to working a seven day week for long periods of time and to a geographically confined existence at that.

My life existed in a triangle comprising my home, my solicitors office and County Hall. Thus it was that I came to live in "Six Mile Triangle".

As a footnote to these County Council episodes I had occasion, shortly after becoming leader, to give a rather challenging exercise in precis to the County's officials. It is reproduced below.

The Bible in short

The following article, summarising the message of the Bible in 300 words, originally appeared in the local government chronicle for 23 September 1977. The author was at that time Leader of the West Midlands County Council, now M.P for Solihull, and the purpose of the article was to encourage local government officers to "cut their reports to the bone" avoiding windy verbiage.

Commencing with an allegoric description of the Creation, at once simple and awesome, the Old Testament presents the fundamental statements of the Law of Israel, as contained in the Pentateuch of their great leader Moses, distilled essentially into the Ten Commandments.

The teaching of these stern disciplines is continued through the histories of 'Judges, Kings and Chronicles' and developed into the experiences of the Chosen People, frequently under hardship and captivity, encouraged, warned and guided by their prophets. Notable amongst these are Elijah, Isaiah and Daniel of whom the latter two in particular portend the coming of a Messiah who will be the Saviour of mankind.

The first verse of the New Testament states that it is "the book of the generation of Jesus Christ". Implicitly he is the Messiah. His ancestry is traced to the Patriarchs of the Old Testament. The enduring story of his birth, upbringing and ministry unfolds through four commentaries. Even to the sceptic who might be tempted to discount the miracle working of this man of God, the impact of his message is impossible to deny. It is best exemplified by his rationalisation of the 10 cardinal points of the old Law into two fundamental precepts: love of God and love of neighbour.

Challenged to define 'neighbour', Jesus Christ offers, as explanation, the Parable of the Good Samaritan which arguably could serve as a counsel of 'Christian' behaviour even if nothing else survived.

It is partly Jesus' ability to reason against an atrophied moral establishment, itself subject to Roman military occupation, that makes him the hope of the oppressed and a source of anxiety to the authorities. Disdaining the immediacy of popular power, Jesus allows himself to be subjected to a trumped-up trial (a satisfaction to the occupied orders and an expedient to the military governorship). He is convicted and crucified, so we are told, only to rise from the dead after three days, offering symbolically the reward of eternal life to the faithful.

The remainder of the New Testament is an anthology of the activities, correspondence and revelations of those galvanised by the events described, serving to witness the dramatic and rapidly widening influence of the life and death of Christ on a civilisation hardly adjusted or receptive at that time to the widescale communication or dissemination of the unorthodox. The influence however persists undiminished, and apparently immutably relevant, despite the subsequent passage of two thousand years.

John M Taylor.

Chapter 16

The European Parliament – Part 1

"Where are the Hapsburgs, the Wellingtons and the Bismarks? They're all here, all duly elected". (Walter Cronkite for CBS 1979)

As 1979 approached, a year in which there had to be a General Election, I had not got a winning seat for Westminster and was not inclined to lose again. But another prospect offered itself. Since 1977 I had been thinking of the first direct elections to the European Parliament also due to be held in 1979. But whereas we did not then know, probably Prime Minister Jim Callaghan didn't either, the exact date of the General Election, we *did* already know that the European Elections in the United Kingdom were to be on Thursday 7 June 1979 with counting on Sunday 10 June 1979. We also knew that they were to be conducted as first-past-the-post elections in single member macro constituencies in Great Britain consisting of six, seven or eight Westminster constituencies rafted together to form one European Constituency. Each such contest would thus produce one winner who would be the Member of the European Parliament (MEP) for that constituency. Northern Ireland was to be a single three-member constituency.

My Party had begun to plan the selection of candidates. European Constituency Councils were set up, to match the European Constituencies, with equal representation on them from each of the Westminster Constituency Associations within that European Constituency's boundaries.

It was quite logical really and beyond reproach as a piece of democracy. In each of the European Constituencies the Conservative selection panels were ready, and a list of approved Conservative European Parliamentary candidates was being assembled who could apply to them. As usual I had been refused the list but an heroic effort on the part of Sir Fred Hardman, who had always been a good friend, never more so, squeezed a success out of my appeal against refusal.

I was in the game.

Towards the end of 1978, briefing meetings were held for the guidance of the selectors. Sir Herbert Redfern addressed a West Midlands Conservative Area Meeting at "The Swan", a well known local hotel in Yardley, Birmingham. Lindsay Allinson and Sue Slesser were both there as agents doing the stewarding, both stunningly attractive. That distraction

Please Stay To The Adjournment

partially overcome, I listened to what was, for me, the most important thing that Sir Herbert had to say: "In this selection we will not be looking for local credentials, we will be looking instead for wider experience ...European credentials...".

I hadn't got any.

It made sense, I suppose, but it was no good to me. Every credential I had was local: birth, education, residence, electoral experience, representative sport and my professional working life.

I was not dismayed or discouraged. In fact I thought Sir Herbert might be right in the absolute "blue chip" unloseable Tory seats where the selectors might be able to reflect on the relative merits of a former British Ambassador (Sir Fred Warner), a former President of the National Farmers' Union (Sir Henry Plumb) or a former Chairman of the National Economic Development Council (Sir Fred Catherwood). They all made it, by the way, in Somerset, Cotswolds and Cambridgeshire, respectively.

But in the more marginal seats and, with hindsight, the definition of "favourable marginal" came to be super-abundant in the Tories favour (we won Merseyside!), I felt that a claim to localness and a pledge to protect "our interests", asserted in Strasbourg and Brussels and re-stated stridently back home, could go down well. In this thinking I can modestly claim to have anticipated the successful themes of still-to-be Prime Minister Margaret Thatcher.

I applied for three candidacies: Birmingham South, from which I subsequently withdrew, Midlands Central, which included the Solihull Constituency, and also Midlands East, a hybrid seat in the sense that it was part Warwickshire and part Leicestershire. Likewise, in regional terms, it was part West Midlands and part East Midlands. It included the Meriden parliamentary half of the Borough of Solihull. As such it included Hampton-in-Arden, so it included my birthplace. I could claim to be a native.

The first of these to select was Midlands Central. It was quite the best in terms of a Tory candidature. It included Stratford-upon-Avon as well as Solihull. John de Courcy Ling, a diplomat, was chosen as the Conservative candidate and went on to win by a very large margin even by European constituency standards. I think his majority was nearly 50,000.

It was an interesting selection. When they reduced the field to five, I had come sixth. One dropped out for whatever reason, success or preference elsewhere almost certainly, and I came back in. When they reduced the field to three I came fourth. Another dropped out likewise for whatever reasons and I came back in and ultimately finished second.

The author wearing his father's Home Guard cap and pack (probably 1944).

Young cricketer at Eversfield 1954 (the white cap denotes "colours").

Bromsgrove School 1st XI Cricket 1960. The author is seated far left.

I

Leader of West Midlands County Council 1977 (on the author's right and left are Sir Anthony Beaumont Dark and the late David Bevan, who also became MPs).

Campaigning for the European election with Edward Heath (1979).

The author in the European Parliament.

The European Democratic Group (very largely British Conservatives) in Strasbourg with the Prime Minister.

An introduction to the Pope as an M.E.P. during 'Study Days' in Rome (November 1980).

An election photograph taken with the prime minister shortly before the 1983 General Election.

Candid Camera 22 November 1988 prior to the State Opening in the Commons.

An agreeable conversation with the Duke of Edinburgh at an Outward Bound reception.

A return to Eversfield Preparatory School for Prize Giving (1991).

As a Government Whip outside the Chief Whips address in Downing Street.

The author with Congressman Ben Gilman (Capitol Hill - September 1989).

The Whips Office entertains the Prime Minister to dinner (inside 12 Downing Street).

The Household Officers about to leave for Buckingham Palace the author (Vice-Chamberlain) the late David Lightbown (Comptroller) and Alastair Goodlad (Treasurer).

In morning dress with wand as Vice-Chamberlain.

BUCKINGHAM PALACE

17th March, 1992.

Dear John,

The Queen read what may have been your valedictory dispatch, with her usual pleasure and interest, but with a tinge of sadness. You have performed your duties as Her Majesty's Vice Chamberlain elegantly, tactfully, and with an eye to just those areas of House of Commons business which are of interest to The Queen and her Private Secretaries.

Her Majesty sends you her warm thanks for all the hard labour you have undertaken on her behalf, and her best wishes for the future, whatever the next month brings.

I would like to add also the thanks and good wishes of Ken Scott, Robin Janvrin and myself. We have enjoyed having you as our friend and colleague very much indeed.

(ROBERT FELLOWES)

John Mark Taylor, Esq., MP.

A Valedictory Acknowledgement from the Palace (17 March 1992).

The 1983 intake ten years on with John Major outside Number 10. The author is second from left.

Back at the Whips Office in Opposition (the leader of the party, William Hague, joining the Office in this group photograph).

The Queen opens the new Touchwood Development in Solihull (2nd July 2002).

The author with the Chief Rabbi (centre) at the 25th Anniversary of the Solihull and District Hebrew Congregation (27th October 2002). © Photo Des Gershon/CIP Editorial Images.

Petra: photo by the author (1993).

The author pictured in Solihull High Street. © Photo Des Gershon/CIP Editorial Images.

Chapter Sixteen – The European Parliament - Part 1

Losing to John Ling but beating Trixie Gardner. I made an important decision. I went into the hall, I was entitled to do so anyway as a member of the Solihull delegation on the floor, and congratulated the victor as he entered after me and I remembered to kiss his wife. He made his acceptance speech and in a kind (I think) remark about me said that (he thought) my future would be at Westminster. Perhaps it was dismissive but I will give him the benefit of the doubt.

Well I had lost that one. Midlands East European Constituency Council had still to select. Not for the first time I had a long conversation at my little bachelor home with my friend Mike Ellis. He was a good friend and a shrewd political adviser. At the time he was an elected Solihull Councillor and a senior officer in the Solihull Conservative Association. We looked at the Midlands East European Constituency. In terms of Westminster representation, it comprised at that time (but with a General Election approaching): Meriden (Labour held), Nuneaton (Labour held), Rugby (Labour held), Loughborough (Labour held) and Bosworth and Blaby (both Conservative held). I dare say Mike and I drank the best part of a bottle of whisky before I had decided to go for it and to abandon Birmingham South where I had reasons to believe I could get the nomination but where I did not then think the Conservatives would win.

I went for the nomination in Midlands East and won it. But not without a bruising questioning from Nigel Lawson (now Lord Lawson), then MP for Blaby, who was the conservative Member of Parliament allocated to the European candidate selection process.

The European election, naturally enough, only really got under way after the General Election of 3 May 1979 which brought Margaret Thatcher to power.

Jim Callaghan had arranged that the General Election would be held on the same day as the local elections. For that reason, not least, the election effort of all the parties' usual political activists had been immense. We had won the General Election and done well in the coincident local elections. The question then arose which of the two principal Parties would have the will, energy and commitment to fight the European elections. The answer to this question was soon clear. Rather like at the conclusion of the annual boat race between Oxford and Cambridge Universities, if you asked each of the crews to row an extra mile only the winners could do it. We rowed the extra mile and I have to say that I was almost unresisted. I met Conservative voters who were quite prepared to come out again and I met Labour voters who said they were not interested. I was accompanied on every sally into the field by a good number of local supporters whichever of the six constituencies I was in. They thought it was fun. We would stop for lunch in a local pub. There were jokes and laughter. I got the impression that my Labour opponent Terry O'Sullivan was coming up from London and returning on a daily basis and was exhausting himself. His early confidence, when he treated me patronisingly, was soon to dissolve. On the eve of poll at a joint platform meeting at Loughborough University for the three candidates in our race, he seemed to be accompanied only by Les Huckfield the Labour MP for Nuneaton. I won decisively and became M.E.P. for Midlands East.

Chapter 17

The European Parliament – Part 2

Six Hundred Mile Triangle

The first direct elections to the European Parliament in June 1979 were a resounding success for the British Conservatives. Eighty one seats in the Parliament were allocated to the United Kingdom under the treaties, the same number as France, Italy and West Germany. Of these eighty one, seventy eight had been contested under a first past the post system in mainland Britain (England, Scotland and Wales) whilst three seats had been contested under a proportional system in Northern Ireland treating that province as a single, three-member, constituency.

Of the mainland's seventy eight, the Conservatives won sixty whilst Labour won seventeen and the Scottish National Party won one. In Northern Ireland my namesake John Taylor won one of the three seats as an Ulster Unionist. Throughout the early years of the directly elected European Parliament he was to sit in our Group with full voting rights. So did two Danish Conservative MEPs and, initially, a third Danish MEP from a compatible part of the spectrum of Danish party politics. At a very early meeting of the Group it was decided that the Group itself should be named "The European Democratic Group" or the E.D.G. as it was more simply and commonly referred to. We were registered as the European Democratic Group with the Parliamentary authorities. We were the third largest Group after the Socialists and the Christian Democrats.

The size and composition of registered Groups matter very considerably in the European Parliament. Under the d'Hondt allocation system, much more recently experienced in our own domestic affairs in the allocation of ministerial portfolios in the Northern Ireland Executive, Group size, not least, determined the Group's entitlements. That is to say its entitlements to Chairmanships of committees, places on the Bureau, the number of Quaestors and so on which the Group would have. It also determined the peck order in which the Group was entitled to bid for those positions. Under this system, there was a bias in favour of being bigger. It was not merely better to be bigger. It was much better to be bigger.

In terms of our Group's numbers and size, no one looking at those first direct election results of 1979 to the European Parliament could say that the British Conservatives could possibly have done any better within our own jurisdiction. We had won everything we could possibly have won, even Merseyside, as I have said elsewhere.

Where we might have done better was in attracting and recruiting other, likeminded, MEPs within the Parliament from other nations. Such recruiting, had it happened, would have helped us not merely to gain numbers but also to gain additional nationalities which also, by itself, paid dividends under the d'Hondt system.

The Group, after all, was not merely a British Group but a Group within the European Parliament. Nor did the name "Conservative" resonate very well in the cultures of other member countries. This underlay the adoption of the anodyne name of our Group. We wanted to be open to others in the competitive business of membership recruitment. MEPs from other member states might be deterred from joining a Group with Conservative in its name. Meanwhile, they couldn't possibly join a Group with British in its name.

Among some members of the Group, myself not included, there remained always the residual attraction of our Group's merging with the Christian Democrats to make a Mega Group, with huge entitlements, from which we could have drawn our share of the spoils.

This theme was to play, unsuccessfully, throughout my five years in the European Parliament and was to be resolved, long after I left, in favour of those who *did* want to join with the Christian Democrats and who, after the 1999 European elections were to see this expressed in membership of the largest ever single Group in the European Parliament with the advantages that went with that in the European Parliament itself alongside, paradoxically, considerable presentational disadvantages at home.

But going back to the earliest stages, the E.D.G. met for the first time, as such, in Luxembourg in July 1979. I arrived slightly late, having had to settle my exits from the Leadership of the West Midlands County Council. It was almost immediately clear to me that this was the most talented debating society of which I had ever been a member. To this day I think that remains my judgement. The Conservatives elected to the European Parliament in those first direct elections were the most eclectically talented Group of people that I have ever had the privilege of belonging to. [1]

Early in 1979, the Leader of the Conservative Party, Margaret Thatcher, soon to become our Prime Minister, had simply announced that Jim Scott-Hopkins would be our Leader. She was in a position to do so. We had not, as the British members of the EDG, any other custom or any other

---

1. In his Address at the Memorial Service for Madron Seligman (also had been one of our number in the original EDG) on 30th October 2002 Lord Jenkins of Hillhead said: "...that British Tory group in the 1979 Parliament was one of exceptional quality...".

Chapter Seventeen – The European Parliament - Part 2

experience of working with one another to presume to have a better idea or to presume that the appointment of our Leader might actually be in our gift rather than her's. It was only later that we began to assume that we might be an electoral college in ourselves and that we could make our own decisions. In the short term we contentedly accepted Jim's leadership. We elected a Bureau, the management executive of the group, and Jim Scott-Hopkins appointed his Spokesmen.

Rather to my surprise, but not to my displeasure, he appointed me Group Budget Spokesman. Since almost nothing in European Parliamentary deliberation was without budgetary implication, I found myself involved in almost everything. It was a huge job. It was the steepest learning curve I have ever known. As I approached my thirty eighth birthday I set myself the biggest single reading course of my life. The Group contained clever men. I was determined that, on my subject, I would be ahead of them or, at the very least, abreast of the best.

I served as the Group's Spokesman on the European Parliament's Budget Committee and also as a member of the Budgetary Control Committee. The Budgetary Control Committee is the Parliament's audit committee which, in my opinion, has never fully exercised its considerable powers. The fact is that the European Parliament was brought into being with powers that national parliaments had taken centuries to gain: power over the budget, power over legislation, power over the executive. So far it has failed to use the potential given to it. Rather than "crunch the numbers" over the probity of Commission expenditure on detailed areas of the Common Agriculture Policy or Third World Aid, the European Parliament, all too often, found itself seduced into populist debates on things over which it had precious little influence or control such as apartheid, the 'Contras', or the situation in Chile.

Of course the European Parliament's time would be better spent in hounding scrutiny of the Commission's budget in all its aspects. That would be a real exercise of power. That would be seriously convertible to constituent and electoral approval. But that would involve an awful lot of hard work!

In our very earliest group meetings it had been agreed, and I had argued for it, tellingly, that the group Leader should make the initial dispositions of place and office within the Group. After all we hardly knew each other whereas Jim Scott-Hopkins did have Margaret Thatcher's imprimatur. I had also argued that this should be a temporary expedient and that democracy should prevail later.

Indeed it did and the Group, working together and knowing itself better, collectively and individually, was to move toward the inevitable assumption that it could elect not only its own officers but its own Leader. In 1981 the Group held elections. Having been budget spokesman of the Group for almost two years I decided to stand for election to the Group's Bureau which was the inner cabinet of our affairs. The constitution of the Group was such that the person who gained most votes in the Bureau elections would be Deputy Leader of the Group. I gained most votes and became Deputy Leader. I could afford a smile in that without a desperate struggle, fought on my behalf, it has to be said, rather than by me, I would not even have been on the list of those eligible for election to the European Parliament in the first place.

I should add a word about the working of the European Parliament. In many ways it resembled an English County Council, its many languages notwithstanding. The main work of the Parliament was done by committees composed of M.E.P.s appointed to them and devoted to subject areas of deliberation and report. There was a Budget Committee, an Agriculture Committee, a Third World Aid Committee (by whatever name) and so on. Their reports were presented for discussion and decision to plenary sessions of the Parliament meeting as a whole, once a month. So far, so much like an English County Council, as I have said.

But the overall culture of the European Parliament was of consensus politics not adversarial politics, as we are used to. So when 'emergency' debates loomed, as they often did, on 'great issues of the day' efforts would be made to find a common position that everyone could vote for. The accredited spokesmen of the various Groups would scurry about negotiating a text with sufficient accommodations to please everyone or, at least, not endanger their hostility. The result, invariably, was a formal resolution of piety, weak tea and platitudes, scarcely startling the diminishing press corps accredited to follow the European Parliament's affairs. What a contrast with the House of Commons where, as I knew, though I was not yet a Member, issues were settled adversarily in divisions on clearly set questions with a determinant outcome in which there would be winners and defeated losers.

I met very many interesting people in the European Parliament. One of the first Vice Presidents of the Parliament, later to be its President, was Pierre Pflimlin who stylishly combined that Office with being Mayor of Strasbourg. He had been Prime Minister of France's Fourth Republic for 17 days.

Then there was Otto von Hapsburg, fluent in five languages, whose contributions to our affairs almost out- performed the lustre of his name.

A Vice-Chairman of our Budget Committee was the Italian Communist Altiero Spinnelli, both jolly and sagacious, who had been incarcerated by

Chapter Seventeen – The European Parliament - Part 2

Mussolini during the Second World War. A sprinkling of former national Government Leaders, apart from Pflimlin, were with us in the early stages, notably Willi Brandt, Jacques Chirac and Leo Tindemans. Perhaps it was pity that Edward Heath was not there. Barbara Castle was.

The European Parliament in my time held its committee meetings in Brussels, its plenary weeks in Strasbourg and also in Luxembourg. During plenary weeks we held our Group pre-meetings in those locations, prior to and in preparation for the Parliament's business. But at other times we generally held our Group meetings in London and, in deference to our Danish colleagues, occasionally in Copenhagen. Even more occasionally we would hold Study Days which could be in any "seat" of the Parliament or any capital city within the Community. I remember one such event in Rome, when I met the Pope, and another in Athens. For me this was a much broader view of the world.

From being a prisoner in six mile triangle I was at large in six hundred mile triangle and scarcely confined to that.

Chapter 18

The European Parliament – Part 3

A Constituency Episode

Jack Jones was a man I came to respect and admire. He was secretary of the North West Leicestershire branch of the National Union of Mineworkers (N.U.M.). He had helped to organise the campaign of my Labour opponent in the European election of June 1979.

Not very long after being elected I rang him to say that whilst I appreciated that I was not his preference I was, of course the MEP for Midlands East and, as we both knew, for a five-year term. He did not need reminding by me that there were live issues concerning coalmining both in his branch area and, correspondingly, in my Euro constituency. I suggested that a meeting might be useful. He received this suggestion courteously but without commitment and told me that he would be consulting some of his members and that he would shortly come back to me.

Within a few days he duly did so. He suggested that on a mutually convenient date he would convene those of his members, who were interested, in the Chamber of the Local District Council. He would take the Chair and I would address his members and then answer their questions.

A date was soon agreed. The meeting was to be held between 10.00 am and 12.30pm at Coalville, appropriately enough, on Saturday, 15 September 1979.

All went according to plan. Jack Jones chaired the meeting scrupulously. I addressed his members. They put questions to me bluntly and firmly but entirely fairly. Jack Jones, utterly in charge, decided when the meeting should close and duly closed it.

What followed was unexpected. He explained to me that after such a meeting it was conventional to go to the pub across the road. I was happy about this and soon found myself with a pint in my hand surrounded by the informal friendliness of those who had been questioning me. A couple of drinks later - I was worried about the breathalyser - Jack Jones again called the assembled company to order and said that he had a presentation to make. A dutiful silence followed - it was perfectly obvious how much his members respected Jack Jones - and he presented me with a Miner's Lamp. It remains one of my most treasured possessions.

Jack Jones went on to oppose Arthur Scargill in the industrial troubles that followed in the mining industry.

Chapter 19

An Interlude On Cricket

'If everything else in this nation of ours were lost but cricket – her Constitution and the laws of England – it would be possible to reconstruct from the theory and practice of cricket all the eternal Englishness which has gone to the establishment of that Constitution and the laws aforesaid.' Cricket 1930 by Neville Cardus

'Explaining cricket to an American' has become a minor figure of speech in our language, a proverbial impossibility.

On the rare occasions that I have attempted this challenge, I think I can say that it is actually achievable to a modest extent, in conversation with a willing and interested listener. Nor need the explanation be so extended as to threaten that willingness or interest.

There are some qualifications. Firstly it helps enormously to be at a match watching a game of cricket being played or at the very least watching cricket coverage on television though that is considerably inferior for the purpose. In the absence of either I would not attempt it at all. Nor would I attempt it unless the American in question had a pretty good knowledge of baseball and at least a passing knowledge of tennis.

This last qualification may surprise you. At some stage in the explanation, certainly not right at the beginning, the American, with his or her given knowledge of baseball, in which the pitch is always a full toss, must be introduced to the concept of the striker receiving a ball that has already bounced on the ground before it reaches him and which is rising when it arrives. This is not a feature of baseball but it is the precise experience of the receiver of service in tennis and thus can be introduced as a not completely alien idea.

That is the only role that tennis plays in my explanation but I think it is quite a useful one and a debating argument could be made that bowling in cricket is more akin to serving in tennis than to pitching in baseball.

The real nub of the matter comes back to the baseball analogy. As ever when explaining something difficult, it is important to build on the confidence of the listener by starting with as many similarities or familiarities as possible. Only from that established platform can the, still willing we hope, American be invited to consider some of the dissimilarities.

Please Stay To The Adjournment

The American must, at some early stage, be invited to contemplate a baseball-like game with two bases not four. There is a familiar batter and catcher at one of those bases and the pitcher's position and the other base are virtually the same. If the American can cross that conceptual hurdle then you are in business.

Next comfort him or her by as much common ground as you can. This is part of the confidence building. Explain that the game is played in episodes called innings. That the job of the pitcher is to try to get the batter out. The job of the batter is to try to score some runs. Big hits can be sensational and count for more runs than more modest efforts. The batter is out if he is caught by a fielder within the bounds of the game. The batter is out if he fails to make his ground when going for a run.

You will have got the idea but you are now into more difficult territory and you must make a judgement as to whether your listener wants to know more. If the American does want you to go on, you could say that there is a version of cricket ('Tip and Run') in which the batter must run if he hits the ball, as in baseball, but in the mainstream cricket game that is a matter for the batter's discretion. In cricket he need not do so if that would be suicidal.

Your most difficult area of explanation, if you have got this far, is dealing with the fact that play behind the wicket is an important part of cricket. This is utterly at variance with the diamond layout of a baseball ground where anything 'behind the wicket' is 'foul'. Interestingly before the time of Ranji[1], and even into his time, deliberate play behind the wicket in cricket was considered by some to be unseemly.

But I end my pretentious master-class at this stage. You can make of it what you will.

I set out to make my own first cricket bat at the age of about four or five. I took a short thick plank. I made two limited cuts down from the top to narrow it and two cuts in from the side to meet those cuts and I had a handle and a blade. My father saw what I was doing and asked me about it. I told him I was making a cricket bat. I do not recall that he registered any particular interest. But the following day he simply gave me a proper cricket bat, appropriate for a small boy, and a set of stumps and a ball. I did not know then that cricket was an abiding passion of my father nor did I know that it was to become one of mine. Only golf, politics and women were ever to get on to the same shortlist.

My cricket at school has been mentioned elsewhere. In the summer holidays, in addition to beginning to play club cricket at the weekends for

---

1. Ranjitsinhji, Kumar Shri, afterwards H.H. the Jam Saheb of Nawanagar (India, Camb. Univ., Cambridge and Sussex).

Chapter Nineteen – An Interlude On Cricket

Hampton-in-Arden, initially in the second XI, I played mid-week matches for Knowle & Dorridge Colts XI and gained some valuable experience by doing so because we played a strong fixture list against good boy players who, in the early years, were invariably older than me. In my final year for Knowle & Dorridge Colts I captained the team and greatly enjoyed the experience. I remain grateful to Knowle & Dorridge.

I then played my club cricket for twenty years including five games for the MCC. My real aptitude was as a bowler. I was accurate and I consolidated that by practising assiduously. I could bat a bit and had a fairly sound defence but if the situation or the mood required I could alternate with fairly reckless hitting. I was a natural number 6 or number 7 or otherwise an opener. To my regret I never made a century. I got out once on 79, quite unnecessarily, when a century was there for the taking on an easy pitch with plenty of time in hand. I have had even more time to think about that innings since and how I might have finished it off. Such is life.

On 29th August 1969, rather later, I captained a Hampton-in-Arden team by a twist of fate against a Knowle & Dorridge XI and won the toss. We batted first and declared on 199, a little while before tea, setting what the opposition conceded was a fair target. When it was their turn to bat, Knowle & Dorridge had reached 125 for 5 before I put myself back on to bowl having already taken three of the five wickets that had fallen.

The first ball that I bowled was straight and the batsman played it straight back down the pitch to me. With the second ball I bowled him. With the third bowl I bowled the next batsman. With the fourth ball I bowled the next batsman. With the next ball, the fifth, I bowled the next batsman. My sixth ball was straight and the batsman played it straight down the pitch to me. I had taken four wickets in four balls, all bowled. Our opponents had subsided from 125 for 5 to 125 for 9 in one over. It was a four wicket maiden and four wickets in four balls. I still have the ball. It has a silver plate on it. It is my ultimate affirmation that I could bowl six straight balls in succession. The evidence is that I hit the stumps four times in a row and I believe that the first and sixth balls of that over were straight as well.

Another cricket recollection is of what I consider to be, in its own way, an equal bowling performance.

It was to be in a match between Hampton-in-Arden Cricket Club and Netherton Cricket Club which was in the Dudley East parliamentary constituency where I fought in those two General Elections of 1974. Possibly the best batting wicket I ever bowled on. I took no wickets at all.

I simply bowled thirty overs, unchanged, for seventy runs. Oddly enough, whilst unrewarded by wicket - taking, that may have been my best piece of controlled bowling and I did it in borrowed boots!

I gave up cricket at the age of thirty six on the advice of an orthopaedic surgeon who was to become a friend of mine, John Polyzoides. My left knee had begun to trouble me. He examined my knee with minute professional care and at the end asked me for how long I had played cricket. I told him I had played club cricket for twenty years. Tellingly he asked me if I had enjoyed it. Leaving aside what my reply might have been, he offered me the prospect of walking, at the age of seventy, with or without a stick. I took the message. With the exception of playing five qualifying games for the M.C.C., which secured me my treasured membership of that illustrious Club, that was the end of playing regular cricket for me.

I was content. There were other things in my life by now. At the time of writing I walk without a stick. I have the ball with which I took four wickets in four balls with a final return in that match of 7-29.

Chapter 20

Member of Parliament

Nunc Dimittis

In 1982 Percy Grieve, the sitting Conservative Member of Parliament for Solihull, announced that he would not be seeking re-election.

The Solihull constituency had been formed in 1945. Sir Martin Lindsay had been the M.P. from 1945 until 1964 when he had been succeeded by Percy. Both had sat for nineteen years. Solihull had only had two Members of Parliament. For most of that time the parliamentary constituency had been co-terminus with the municipality of Solihull. But Peter Walker's enlargement of the Borough of Solihull in 1973 rendered the parliamentary seat of the same name less than the whole Borough but in 1982 the parliamentary constituency still represented a territory evoked by the name of Solihull.

The Conservative parliamentary candidacy for this constituency was a great prize as it always had been.

The Conservative Association was understandably exercised by the anticipation of the selection procedure to find Percy Grieve's successor and the prospect of the conferral of its greatest prize.

When the vacancy was notified to Central Office and when, in turn, Central Office circulated the Candidates' List that Solihull was selecting, there was a huge response. I was, of course, totally aware of what was going on and the challenge was, I suppose, to contain myself. Fortunately my travels as an MEP coupled with the demands of my law practice gave me respectable distance from the Association's affairs and also some authority. My C.V. which had increasingly developed since my election as a councillor eleven years before was, by now, effectively as good as anyone's. It contained the leadership of the second largest local authority in the country and deputy leadership of the Conservative group in the European Parliament. Thanks to Dudley East, it had the credential of having fought twice for Parliament before. Then I got lucky. After nineteen years of Sir Martin Lindsay and nineteen years of Percy Grieve, there was a strong sentiment among the selectors for a local man this time. As I was subsequently to learn from Peter Mitchell OBE, then very influential in the affairs of Solihull Conservative Association, I led the field as the Selection Committee reduced some 250 applications to 20. The twenty were called for interview and reduced to four. The other three were Eric Forth, Andrew Mackay and Charles Wardle, all of whom were to be selected for good Conservative seats prior to the 1983 General Election. The four of us then went before the Executive Council and I very nearly got more votes than the other three combined on the first ballot. A couple of votes would have done it but I won outright on the second ballot and was to go before a General Meeting of the Association for adoption. These days no General Meeting would settle for a choice of one out of one and even then there was some dispute about that prospect. I spent some very anxious days indeed as the possibility circulated of a motion of 'reference back' of the entire selection procedure. I escaped for the weekend to Bath.

The General Meeting soon followed and fortunately the line held against what proved in the end to be only a modest level of dissent. Then the customary unanimity vote was carried. Things settled down. I had the nomination that I had wanted more than almost anything in my life.

The permitted life span of the then current Westminster Parliament, having been elected in May 1979, extended to an equivalent date in 1984 which would have coincided almost exactly with the expiry of my five year term in the European Parliament. But Margaret Thatcher, instinct perfect as it was to remain almost to the end of her reign, went to the electors in June 1983. Labour was in a hell of a mess anyway and the Iron Lady scored a monumental triumph with a majority of 143. The Election in Solihull was unremarkable. The Alliance, as it then was, scored quite well but Labour had a disaster and lost its deposit. The only time it has ever done so in Solihull. I was returned. I took off my Conservative rosette at the declaration, as I always do, before making my acceptance speech. This has always been symbolic to me. It marked the moment when I ceased to be a partisan candidate and assumed the Membership of Parliament for the seat I had always wanted to represent. I had wanted to be an MP, above all I had wanted to be the MP for Solihull.

It had come true. I recited the Nunc Dimittis.

Chapter 21

Back Bencher and Committees

'The important thing about the House of Commons is being there':
Benjamin Disraeli

On election to the House of Commons as part of the vast new conservative intake of 1983, I was scarcely expectant of any preferment and still in the contented, Nunc Dimittis, mood of simply having got there. But I did seek to be occupied, extended even, and got myself appointed to the House of Commons Select Committee on the Environment. This proved to be a good move. Under the industrious chairmanship of Sir Hugh Rossi, the Committee became significant in the affairs of that Parliament not least on account of the number of its Reports which came to be debated on the floor of the House of Commons and the notice taken of them by the Government. This was a serious test of the virility of a Select Committee.

One of the most important works we undertook was our Report on 'Acid Rain'. This was very topical at the time and a serious subject. The assumption was that as our society increasingly produced oxides of nitrogen from vehicle emissions and oxides of sulphur from coal-burning power stations, these releases into the atmosphere were returning to earth, in rainfall, as dilute but significant nitric acid and sulphuric acid.

Our enquiries were directed to understanding whether this was indisputable and if so what effect it was having on fresh water systems, trees and buildings. We took evidence from experts and had our own professional advisers seconded to the Committee. We also travelled to Scandinavia, the Black Forest and Cologne to see fresh-water acidification, which was both alleged and disputed. We saw damage to woodland and damage to buildings attributed to acid rain.

A very significant report emerged from this process which was the unanimous finding of the Committee and which contained some eighty four recommendations for the amelioration of this harmful process. Seventy nine of our recommendations were implemented by the Government. This was Select Committee work at its very best and its most impressive.

During the same Parliament I served on a number of Standing Committees as well. It was all good training for me in the work of the House.

Towards the end of the 1983-87 Parliament two surveys appeared, one in The Guardian and the other in the Today newspaper. One was concerning the most assiduous attenders of committees in the House and the other was as to the most assiduous voters in the division lobbies.

Out of six hundred and fifty members, I came fourth in the first of these and seventh in the second. Naturally enough I used these findings in my own favour at the end of that Parliament, in my election address in the 1987 General Election.

There is a particular memory deriving from our travels in pursuit of evidence for our Acid Rain Report. We went to Cologne to inspect alleged damage to the fabric of Cologne Cathedral. Incidentally, I had to be helped down from the roof of Cologne Cathedral. I had never had much of a head for heights. This one proved too much for me.

Anyway, we made the journey on a flight from London to the airport which serves both Cologne and Bonn. I was seated next to Reg Hobson, the Clerk of the Select Committee, who was shortly to reach retirement. As we neared our destination the usual indicators came on in the cabin of the aircraft ordering No Smoking and telling us to fasten our seat belts. As Reg and I were buckling up he looked to me quite casually and said "John, the last time I made this approach (to Cologne) was in a Lancaster."

I asked him about this again later and he described the immense inferno below. He told me that, after releasing their bombs, the first instinct of the bomber crew was to get away from the fire. But this was a vital moment when that first instinct was positively dangerous and a crucial discipline had to prevail to set course not merely to get away from the fire but to get away on the right bearing for the shortest journey home for which there was enough fuel in the aircraft but not much more.

But I digress. There was, of course, much more to my work on the back benches in my first Parliament than Committee service. All of the new Conservative intake of 1983 attended Question Time in the House at 2.30pm everyday without fail. There were two real reasons for this both of which were competitive. We wanted to get noticed and we wanted to learn and practice the skills of parliamentary questions as fast as we could. It was competitive, not least because there were so many of us and, because if some other new Tory MP got up and took his or her chance, then maybe you would be denied. The experience was not infrequent of leaving the Chamber at the end of Question Time with that splendid and original question, as you thought, unasked.

Of course, some of us made a fool of ourselves at times and then, not knowing at that stage that it really didn't matter, would feel bad about it for several days until some opposite piece of luck would come along and restore our fragile self esteem.

Chapter Twenty-one – Back Bencher And Committees

Meanwhile this process which seemed so important to us had its constituency side.

Our own party associations and many of our constituents would know that we were new M.P.s. Of course they knew. We felt that they would need to be impressed with a good report of an excellent question here or a weighty contribution to an important meeting there. In all probability the people we were trying to impress were gently amused by all of this but I suspect that they viewed it kindly and may have given us credit for trying and for our energy and enthusiasm.

Your party's own new intake, with which you join the House of Commons, actually remains very important to you throughout your time in Parliament. It remains your intake, your peer group. Whilst the early relationship, in particular, is competitive it is also sustaining as you learn together. In due course this is where most of your closest friends will come from and your confidants, especially in times of difficulty.

In these same early stages you will make your maiden speech. Wise "maidens" will seek neither to be amongst the first nor to be among the last. The maiden speech is unique. By definition you can never make it again or have another go. It is important to get it right. It is well worth thinking about. If you do, it is actually easy. No one will interrupt you. Every subsequent speaker will say how good it was. In terms of difficulty your second speech is much harder.

But in this same competitive spirit we queued up, so to speak, over a period of several weeks to make our maiden speeches. As with our early parliamentary questions members of this intake, no doubt as of every other, would be heard to say "I must get my Maiden to my local paper".

In the evenings I found the various bars of the House of Commons. In my early days the Smoking Room was a daunting place with large and expensive rounds. I was cautious about this. I also avoided the Strangers Bar because it was too noisy and more like a Tap Room. In those days it was called "The Kremlin" because so many traditional old Labour members drank beer there. I was happier in "Annie's Bar" a traditional off-the-record meeting place between M.P.s and accredited lobby correspondents. In "Annie's" the rounds were small and the conversation was confidential by tradition.

After a little experience of the House I came to say that the only two things that had surprised me about the House of Commons were its humour and its focus for tourism from constituents. I hold by those conclusions.

But for drinking in the bars of Westminster, I had no need for training. That aspect of the job came to me quite naturally.

Please Stay To The Adjournment

During the course of my first Parliament there were three occasions when I was unable as a Conservative back bench MP to support the Conservative Government.

I will not deal with these in chronological order but I will mention first, because it is the least complicated, The Shops Bill 1985-86 which was defeated at Second Reading on 14 April 1986. This was a bill designed, permissively, to extend Sunday Trading. A defeat at Second Reading is very unusual. It is almost a collector's item. It was perhaps introduced a little ahead of public acceptability. The arguments behind it were to prevail decisively when the Government and Parliament returned to the matter later in the Thatcher years. At this first time of asking I abstained. I suppose that may be said to be a small part of the reason for the defeat. Later on, in 1994, I, like others, had become convinced and voted in favour of a superior form of the same legislation.

My second rebellion concerned the motor industry generally and my own constituency in particular. It was the matter of the proposed sale of the Rover car division to Ford and the proposed sale of Land Rover to General Motors. Norman Tebbit was Secretary of State for Trade & Industry. With hindsight there was only one virtue in these proposals which was that they predicted a separate destiny for Rover Cars on the one hand and Land Rover on the other. I have since come to realise how important that separation might have been and, indeed, might still be.[1] However, the prospect of control of the largest piece of the economy of Solihull passing to Pontiac, Michigan was simply unacceptable both locally and wider. I joined the rebellion which consisted primarily of West Midlands Members of Parliament such as Anthony Beaumont-Dark (Birmingham Selly Oak), David Bevan (Birmingham Yardley), Iain Mills (Meriden) and Roger King (Birmingham Northfield). I did more national media interviews over this issue than any other as a back bencher. Among those who interviewed me were Robin Day, Jimmy Young and Gordon Clough. It was a very big story and, for me, it was a very big anxiety. A journalist in The Observer said that I would lose my seat over it. He said that he had had this confirmed to him in casual conversations in the Old Colonial Pub in Damson Lane, in Copt Heath Golf Club and in The Avenue Bowling Club and I was able to take some fleeting comfort from writing a published letter back to that newspaper saying that none of these three venues were in my constituency.

Looking back on the Hansard reporting of those events from just the Parliamentary point of view, I am slightly surprised, but reassuringly, by my own vigour in my first Parliament. I raised the matter on the floor of the

---

1. *This written before the events of March 2000 when the destinies of Rover and Land Rover were indeed separated with the latter destined to be part of Ford.*

Chapter Twenty-one – Back Bencher And Committees

House of Commons on quite a large number of occasions. On the 4th February 1986 I put a challenging question to Prime Minister Margaret Thatcher which probably did me personally no good at all. On 5th February the Labour Opposition secured a Supply Day debate on the question in which I got to my feet again and then voted against the Opposition motion but abstained on my own Government's amendment. I raised the matter again on 17th February and on 18th February, participated in David Gilroy-Bevan's Adjournment Debate also on 18th February and intervened again on 19th February on a Private Notice Question raised by John Smith from the Labour Opposition front bench. I would appear to have been at it again on 11th March, 24th April, 14th May, 30th June, 16th July and even yet again on 5th November of that year and yet again on the 28th January 1987.

The extraordinary thing about that rebellion, given a Government majority of 143, was that we won. Land Rover was *not* sold to General Motors. I believe that the presence in the cabinet of Norman Fowler and Peter Walker made the difference. Before the final, to me, favourable decision was made I remember a lengthy conversation, pacing the Committee Corridor with Norman Fowler, who asked me to brief him as extensively as I could about the Land Rover interest which, to me, was the Solihull interest. Frankly I had prepared myself for a steam-rollered defeat of a rebellion of scarcely more than five. I was preparing myself for how to get up again on the other side of being knocked down. At least I knew that I had spoken for my local interest, as I saw it and as many others saw it. But that preparation, surprisingly perhaps, proved unnecessary. The deal was called off. I was amazed. In his entry concerning me in 'Parliamentary Profiles', Andrew Roth has me: "defeating the Government in 1986 over flogging off local Land Rover plant to General Motors"!

I had been part of a winning rebellion. But this informed my thoughts much later when I became a Whip. It also influenced Kenneth Clarke at the beginning of the next Parliament when he asked me to become his P.P.S. when he said "no more rebellions, you understand, no more Land Rover arguments". By then I knew well enough what he meant.

Ironically, Kenneth Clarke was in the Cabinet as number two at the Department of Trade & Industry when I was his P.P.S. early in the next Parliament when both Land Rover and Rover Cars were sold to British Aerospace. I had no objection to that apart from the lingering doubt about whether they would both have actually had better prospects if they had been separated. But it was an English domicile for ultimate decision making and, for a Conservative of my time, it was a progression from being a nationalised industry into the private sector.

But even at the final moments of the sale of Land Rover and Rover Cars to British Aerospace there was a serious glitch. The European Commissioner responsible for Competition, Peter Sutherland, intervened on the question of whether there had been "doucers" (sweeteners) in the deal.

Ministerial Statements were due and expected and in both Houses on the developing situation. The Dti was forced into preparing not one statement but rather three versions. These might have been summarised as "the deal's on", "the deal's off" and "wait a minute, there are further developments". They were known as A, B and C. Things remained uncertain right up to the last minute. Lord Young's delivery of the statement was due to be made at 3.15pm from the Dispatch Box in the Chamber of the House of Lords. Kenneth Clarke's was due to be made at 3.30pm in the House of Commons. We were seated in the House of Commons as Question Time drew to an end. Kenneth Clarke was on the front bench ready to assume the Dispatch Box. As his P.P.S. I was seated immediately behind him. As 3.30pm approached, he turned casually to me and said "pop up to the House of Lords and see which version David Young is delivering". I sprinted like it was "Chariots of Fire" to the bar of the Chamber of the House of Lords and found that Lord Young was delivering version C. I got back to the House of Commons in time to tell Kenneth Clarke that it was version C even as the Speaker called "Mr Secretary Clarke". Ken Clarke simply read version C consistent with what Lord Young had read in their Lordship's House. It was a close call. It was anxious for me. Ken Clarke took it in his stride.

The third and final area where I differed with my own side in that first Parliament was over the abolition of the Greater London Council. Not that I minded the abolition of the GLC and the machinations of Ken Livingstone. The problem for me was that other Conservative interests, including some prominent Birmingham Conservatives, wanted to abolish the six provincial Metropolitan County Councils as well as the GLC and at the same stroke and in this cause they used the same arguments for the abolition of the 'Mets' as those being used for the abolition of the GLC.

I found this quite unconvincing.

I personally believed that the provincial Metropolitan County Councils were worthwhile and were capable of achieving strategic purposes with democratic authority. I had, after all, been leader of one of them.

Interesting things emerge from this limited opposition by me. I was, as I have said, not opposed to the abolition of the GLC but I was opposed to the abolition of the provincial Metropolitan County Councils.

I wrote a published letter to The Times in this cause and my views were well known locally. Then I got an interesting insight into the workings of

Chapter Twenty-one – Back Bencher And Committees

the Whips Office. They asked me if I would like to go and see the responsible minister and have a glass of sherry with him to see whether he could persuade me of his view or, alternatively, whether I could persuade him of mine. I did this. Indeed I went through every step recommended to me by the Whips Office to see if some kind of resolution could be achieved as to how I might vote on the ultimate question.

Although every courtesy was observed, no change in position was achieved either by me or by the minister representing the Government's position.

Then the Whips told me that they might not need me on the night of the vote in question. They asked me whether I felt I had made my position clear enough nationally and locally. I said I felt I had. They then asked me, in those circumstances, whether I felt it necessary to speak again against the Government's proposals in the House. I said I did not. They asked me next how important I thought it was to enter the division lobby against the Government or whether I could abstain.

They added that they had a better idea in any event. Would I go on the night in question and accept a Conservative speaking engagement at Nottingham University, fulfiling a party commitment and releasing Martin Brandon-Bravo, the local MP whose commitment it was, to be at the House to vote for the Government? This looked like a good deal. They also said that, since this speaking engagement in Nottingham was quite late in the week, they would not want me back in the House of Commons until the following Monday. So the deal was that I had stated my case, I would be out the House of Commons at the time of the vote, I would fulfil a Conservative speaking engagement and I could get back to my constituency sooner than I would otherwise have done. I saw all the merits of this and I agreed. It was also a splendid insight into whipping and into the member by member management of a rebellion. I was impressed and I would remember.

Chapter 22

The Whips Office

History - "Snowbound in Arizona"

Immediately following our successful 1987 General Election I had accepted, with great pleasure, the position of Parliamentary Private Secretary (PPS) to Kenneth Clarke who was appointed the No 2 Cabinet Minister in the Department of Trade and Industry with the title of Chancellor of the Duchy of Lancaster under Lord Young as Secretary of State. It was a fascinating experience and Ken Clarke was a wonderful man to work for. Exactly a year later, in a major reshuffle, he was promoted to head his own department, which was what he wanted, at the Department of Health. He asked me if I would come with him, again as his PPS, and I agreed but within the same day we had another conversation in which he asked me what I would *really* like to do and I said I would love to have a spell in the Whips Office. He acknowledged but said no more. He hurried on wherever but certainly in the right direction for the Whips Office if that was where he had decided to go. Within a few hours I was approached by David Lightbown [1], then a fairly senior Whip himself, and told by him, kindly but slightly mysteriously, that he wanted me to participate in a debate on Housing that very afternoon. I told him, as was the case, that Housing wasn't a particularly strong subject of mine and he reminded me, as Whips always do, that there was a briefing note available and the facilities of the library in any event. Something told me it might be a good idea to oblige so I prepared what the Whips always like in these circumstances, a fairly neat little speech capable of running for about 10 minutes. In it, I said that the three staples of life were food, clothing and housing. I went on to say that food and clothing were broadly provided by the private sector (I could have made an exception of the CAP) but that Housing was generally satisfactory in the area of private provision and private ownership but was attended by all sorts of problems in the public, municipal sector. It was anything but a remarkable speech but it created a few flurries on the other side of the Chamber, served its purpose, and I had done as I had been asked. In accordance with the conventions, then observed more carefully than now, I remained in the Chamber to hear subsequent speeches, not least to see if anyone wanted to comment on anything I had had to say. If they did it would be discourteous for me not to be there to hear it or even intervene on a subsequent speaker if he or she

1. M.P. for Staffordshire South East.

Chapter Twenty-two – The Whips Office

took issue with me. So it was that I was "in my place", as we say, on the Conservative Benches after my speech when one of our Whips Messengers came as far into the Chamber as he was allowed, but far enough to catch my attention, and beckoned me. He told me the Chief Whip wanted to see me straight away. I was puzzled because I could think of nothing that I had done which was out of order or might call for rebuke or explanation. I couldn't help feeling that something more interesting was about to happen. I knocked on David Waddington's [2] door and he called me in and invited me to sit down. He was known to be a man of few words. I respected him very much. "We would like you to join the office" he said. I accepted with pleasure and thanked him. "Right, good", he said and his eyes travelled to the door indicating that the interview was over. There was no point in hanging around and it was perfectly clear that there was nothing more to be said. Obedient to my new Chief, I left promptly, and in the same tempo.

Now nobody, to my knowledge, has ever written a history of the Whips Office. Nor will I. Perhaps because the art of whipping needs to be covert and shrouded in a degree of mystery, those who become loyal to its practice and principles are not inclined to breach them. I am such a loyalist myself. But that does not stop me offering my own hunches about the origin of whipping.

For this we need to consider the nature of British politics in the early eighteenth century following the Hanoverian Succession. History tells us that neither George I nor George II could speak English or if they could it was not very well and this significantly contributed to the fact that they did not attend the Council of Ministers. We all know that Walpole accordingly assumed the chair and became, for all practical purposes, our first Prime Minister, recognisable as such in the subsequent writing of our history. I am in no doubt that British politics was pretty rough and ready in those days. The tax-borne appropriations to the Ministers responsible for the functions of the State would almost certainly have passed to the personal account of the responsible Minister and if he did not make himself rich on the margin between what he received and what he disbursed then he was frankly missing the obvious opportunity which being a Minister presented. Now this was clearly a good game for those involved. There were, however, slight difficulties. In order to achieve the necessary Money Votes in the first place, the House of Commons had first to be quorate and then it needed to have within it a majority in favour of the Money Vote in question. Nor was this entirely straight forward. A large number of Members of Parliament would be landed gentlemen with fine estates that needed the benefit of their attention and not merely in the

2. *M.P. for Ribble Valley and Government Chief Whip.*

hunting season. Westminster at the time would have been contrastingly malodorous, unhealthy and quite a dangerous place.

Meanwhile the obvious question, which presented itself to the ministerial elite, was how to get these gentlemen to be in Westminster and more than that to pass through the correct division lobby at the right time. The answer is contained in that splendid euphemism "patronage". Now you can read into that anything you like and, at some stage of the operation, over time, even your most bizarre interpretation will have been right. But the essence of the matter, of course, was money. A knighthood here and there, of course, but the other thing about these country gentlemen was that not a few were strapped for cash. A visit to London could be made worthwhile.

The origin of the word "whipping" is not difficult to see. This is the idiom of the hunt, comfortably familiar to country gentlemen. It is about keeping the pack together and uniting its numbers to good effect. Nor is it entirely surprising that to supervise this operation, the ministerial elite, as I have called them, looked to the Parliamentary Secretary to the Treasury. He had access to what was needed, money. Over time he became known as the Patronage Secretary and in more modern times simply Chief Whip. Even today however, the more elegant speakers in the Chamber of the House of Commons when referring, on the floor, to some expectation of the Chief Whip will refer to him as the Patronage Secretary.

But how was one man to commandeer a majority of how many of the 500 or so turned up? He needed help. He needed staff. In short he needed henchmen, unquestioning of his bidding and determined to get results for him. Nor was that going to be done for nothing. And so I suspect that the Patronage Secretary or even The First Lord of the Treasury (Prime Minister) may have had a conversation with the Monarch. Such a conversation may well have taken place with both sides fully aware of the fact that the Monarch himself had an interest in a successful Money Vote on the Civil List. So, in his own way, the Monarch too would be served by the whipping operation and, reluctantly or otherwise, he ceded to its purposes a small number of non-jobs or sinecures which were in his gift. Some of them had elegant names like Comptroller of the Household. They had long since ceased to entail any work or responsibility. But they carried a salary. The Chief Whip was in business. He could get henchmen and pay them. The quorum and the majority was to be, generally speaking, manageable. Patronage would flow. Ministers would get rich, the King would get his Civil List. The impoverished knights of the shires would be sustained. Effective government was assured. England would be powerful.

Chapter Twenty-two – The Whips Office

When I joined the Whips Office two and a half centuries later things had calmed down a bit.

There were Standing Committees with an inherent government-side majority to be stewarded, a duty roster to be observed, taking one's turn to be in the Chamber of the House to be a discreet floor manager, speakers to be recruited for forthcoming debates where such debates were not already adequately subscribed and voting defaulters to be pursued. In short, all the usual stuff. Whipping at times seemed to me to be all about lists of names.

There is a kind of mythology, which incidentally Whips do nothing to suppress, that whipping is about browbeating, arm twisting, shouting and generally being unpleasant with people to make them do something they would not have done if they had not been set upon.

I am afraid this does not bear very close examination. Whereas there are occasions when aggression and threat have come into play, those occasions are, in my opinion, cases where the proper working of the Whips Office has failed. After all, Members of Parliament are seldom shy people. They are, in my experience, usually fairly self-confident and it is not unusual for them to have quite strong opinions which they have thought about, held to and spoken about publicly and urged on others over a period of time, perhaps a long time. Any idea that they will abandon those views and vote in strict contradiction of them because a Whip comes and shouts at them is nonsense. I don't need to pursue this line of argument. It is obvious. Nor is man-management all that much different in politics from any other walk of life. I allow that in many other occupations there will be the relationship of employer and employee which permits what the lawyers would call "a lawful order". In other words in employment the employee can be given an instruction and in certain extended circumstances non-compliance could lead to dismissal. No such sanction is at the disposal of a Whip. His fellow Member of Parliament, whilst admittedly elected with more or less assent to the same manifesto, is not his employee and cannot be given an order. Indeed it is an interesting question, what is an MP if he is not an employee and to whom is he accountable? All the possible answers to this question come out in the plural. He has lots of accountabilities. But always one of them is to what he sincerely and conscientiously believes to be right.

How then are the Whips to manage their fellow Members of Parliament? I am not going to go much further than this. Leaving aside rogue behaviour by members of your own side which may call for sterner measures, the real answer is that the Whips must keep alongside those MPs for whom they are responsible, at the direction of the Chief Whip, and generally speaking (and this applies for the vast majority of the time) make sure that they are gainfully employed doing useful things that they get some satisfaction from. Then it is necessary to be as accommodating as possible with their particular needs for a bit of time off here and there when a constituency engagement seems more important (to them) than the call of the House on that particular day. In short, a Whip should be as reasonable as possible with his charges in reconciling their needs on the one hand to the overall direction of the Parliamentary Party on the other in the expectation, surprisingly often rewarded, that when the time comes the Member will, in turn, be reasonable to the Whip. "Come", you may say, "There must be more to it than that. Don't fob me off with that soft soap. There are dark arts and you know there are". Okay, if that's the way you want it.

I served as a Government Whip from July 1988 until, and including the General Election of 1992.

I went into the office at the same time as three other new recruits. They were David Heathcoat-Amory, Tom Sackville and Michael Fallon. That was to be our order of seniority in the seniority-conscious Whips Office. The other member of the Lower Office was Stephen Dorrell who was, in turn, senior to us. In the Upper Office were five more senior Whips each carrying the rank of Lord Commissioner of the Treasury plus the Vice Chamberlain of the Household, the Comptroller of the Household and the Deputy Chief Whip who carried the rank of Treasurer of the Household. In a separate, adjoining office was the Chief Whip himself. In my almost four years as a Government Whip I advanced reasonably rapidly and satisfactorily from my point of view. Before long I was head of the Lower Office myself and then moved up, literally, to the Upper Office which was Upper both in the sense of being more senior and in the sense that one had to go up a small flight of steps to reach it from the Lower Office.

Whips in Government are assigned to the various Departments of State both to meet with the Ministers in those Departments at their regular morning meetings known as "Prayers" and to follow and facilitate the progress in the Commons of the various stages of such legislation as the Department was promoting. The Whip in question would also take a particular interest in the conduct of the Parliamentary Question Time of the Departments he worked with and be in attendance at the Back Bench Committee meetings of those party groups whose subject areas were the same as the Department's. Normally no Whip ever followed the affairs of any Department for too long. It was always said, light-heartedly, that this was for fear of the Whip in question "going native". By this was meant becoming too imbued with the culture of the Department such that the Whip might become

Chapter Twenty-two – The Whips Office

uncritical of its performance and fail to spot an alarm of which the Chief Whip should be aware. In my case there was an exception to this on-your-toes re-shuffling of responsibilities because I was Welsh Whip for the whole time of my being a Whip in Government. This was unusual. Not least because I was an Englishman but I think that I gained and held an acceptable level of confidence not only with our limited number of Conservative Welsh MPs but also with Welsh MPs of other parties. It was during this time that I came to work with Peter Walker as mentioned in the opening paragraphs of my chapter about The West Midlands County Council.

Meanwhile my job as Welsh Whip involved me in organising to best advantage the debates in the Welsh Grand Committee. In this I had little difficulty. Peter Walker was superb. Notwithstanding the inherent, large Labour majority in the Welsh Grand Committee, Peter Walker finessed it every time. He always threw them. Despite his absence of a supporting majority, he always got the better of those occasions.

I spent my time as a Lord Commissioner of the Treasury, incidentally signing warrants, from time to time, for gigantic sums of Government money and then, towards the end of July 1990 I was asked to do what I found the least enjoyable of my Whips duties. I became Pairing Whip. In Government this job is effectively about managing the Government's majority. The Pairing Whip alone is responsible for deciding who can be away for whatever reasons and who cannot. There is no court of appeal beyond the Pairing Whip. He must carry it all himself and if it goes wrong it is his fault.

On the lighter side, and there wasn't too much of that, I got an insight into the ingenuity of colleagues' excuses for missing divisions, that is to say failing to vote when they should have done. The best excuses were bold and extravagant. I thought of writing an anthology of such excuses. It remains stillborn but I have its title. It is called "Snowbound in Arizona". This I had from Sir Eldon Griffiths the long-standing MP for Bury St Edmunds. It has all the hallmarks of a great excuse. Self-assured, sweeping, majestic and breath-taking, even Dr Goebbels would have been impressed. What was the next question anyway? Why were you in Arizona? Does it snow in Arizona? How very superior in any case to "funeral of a close relative, old boy, short notice..." or "my Constituency Chairman needed an urgent meeting with me about some important local matters, couldn't really get out of it, meant to ring you but the phones were down". And then all those other ones about the London traffic. Wearily I pass on.

Probably the best job, by far, that I did in the Whips Office took me out of the Pairing Whips job after, for me, a mercifully short time. This was December 1990.

Please Stay To The Adjournment

But then the political scene, at least, changed almost completely. Margaret Thatcher, whom I had supported and served unswervingly was un-horsed and John Major won a leadership contest, which was, of course, a contest to be Prime Minister. That contest was finally down to him or Michael Heseltine or Douglas Hurd. Naturally this was followed by a significant re-shuffle. In the course of this I was promoted within the Whips Office from Pairing Whip to Vice Chamberlain of the Household and for my last sixteen months in the Whips Office, in Government, from December 1990 to April 1992, my duties included the daily reporting of the proceedings of the House of Commons to my Sovereign in a written Message. Pending bankruptcy alone might cause me to reconsider the confidentiality of those texts. I have kept copies of them all. No, on second thoughts, it would not. They would go down with my ship, unread by anyone else.

I had Garden Party responsibilities too and a number of private audiences with Her Majesty as Vice Chamberlain. None of that is for disclosure, of course, except that I have the highest regard for my Sovereign by whose grasp of public affairs and good humour I was always immensely impressed.

I have always considered my best deployment in my Party's cause in the House was as a member of the Whips Office. After the 1992 General Election I was to leave it for the Lord Chancellor's Department.

I was to return to the Conservative Whips Office, five years later, in Opposition, after the great defeat of 1997 (see Chapter 28).

Chapter 23

The Lord Chancellor's Department

Red Boxes

After the pleasantly surprising result had come in for the General Election of 9 April 1992, Privately predicted to me by John Major when I met him at Birmingham airport on the Tuesday before poll, I was having lunch at Da Corrado, my favourite restaurant, with my friend Brian Phillips. It would be the lunchtime of Tuesday 14 April when Helen Collodi, the proprietress, came to me and said there was a call from 10 Downing Street. Belief half suspended, I left the table and Helen asked me if I would like to take the call in her office. I did so. There was a voice on the other end of the telephone, which asked me for a few details about myself, which were clearly a security and identity check. I obviously must have given satisfactory answers because John Major then came on the telephone and said that he would like me to leave the Whips Office and do an entirely new job as Junior Minister to the Lord Chancellor representing the Lord Chancellor's Department in the House of Commons. I was overwhelmed. I simply accepted without asking the rank of the position, which was, not unnaturally, to be Parliamentary Secretary. I concluded the conversation by telling John Major that I would shortly ring the Lord Chancellor himself. I returned to my table with Brian Phillips and told him. A good lunch then briefly got supremely better but ended otherwise earlier than it would have done.

I had things to do.

Curiously this appointment had been anticipated as being imminent in an isolated provincial press notice (I think it was the Birmingham Mail), a mere nine days before the election. It actually predicted that I would be made this minister in the few days that remained before poll. Since the newspaper thought Labour would win, and not without reason, it tipped me as the man about to be the shortest ever serving minister.

I was able to piece together the fact that the Home Affairs Select Committee, very recently taking evidence from the Lord Chancellor, had been considering the usefulness of his Department's having a Junior Minister in the House of Commons. Keith Vaz (LAB, Leicester East), a member of the Committee, had heard my name mentioned informally, by the Lord Chancellor he said, and congratulated me.

Oddly, at about this time, I had received a phone message to ring Downing Street which I did only to be told that there must be some mistake because there was no message for me.

I decided to take all this with a pinch of salt. In any event the press notice appeared on April 1st. I drew my own conclusions, which were no conclusions, anyway we were in mid-election.

But the General Election of 1992 having been surprisingly won by John Major and my Conservative Party, this very appointment actually happened and happened to me.

This remains an entertaining if not very significant mystery or a genuine case of a decision made, very slightly spilt, put on hold, stifled and subsequently implemented.

Anyway I now had the reality.

I headed for London with a view to reporting to the Lord Chancellor himself and the Lord Chancellor's Department generally. I was aware of something that (Lord) Patrick Mayhew had said to me about the Lord Chancellor's Department which was that, whilst all the orthodox opinion was in favour of a Junior Minister being appointed with House of Commons responsibilities, the Old Guard in the Lord Chancellor's Department, that is to say the Civil Servants, had resisted this trenchantly until the end.

There were interesting press commentaries at the time about my appointment, not about me personally but rather more about the position. These were flavoured by the anticipation that my appointment was the beginning of something more fundamental. That the functions of the Lord Chancellor himself might gradually move, via my appointment as a middle-stage, toward House of Commons accountability for his function in the form of a Minister of Justice. I enjoyed reading these articles and was mindful of what F.E. Smith, Lord Birkenhead, had said about the question over seventy years before. After discussing the arguments, that great man had come down in favour of the Lord Chancellor's responsibilities remaining in the House of Lords rather than in the Commons. Nonetheless, not for the first time in my life, I had a novelty on my hands.

On arrival at the Department, I felt myself confronted by a Civil Service, at its most senior levels, which had, in part, come to terms with this new appointment and, in part, not come to terms with it and disposed to fence me in and, by protecting me, protect themselves.

The rooming arrangements of the Lord Chancellor's Department had anticipated that there would be a Junior Minister to the Lord Chancellor. Labour had put it in their manifesto. We had not. Since the general expectation had been that Labour would win the Election arrangements

Chapter Twenty-three – The Lord Chancellor's Department

had gone ahead anyway and thoroughly. There was a suite of rooms for me and a Private Secretary who was designated to me and in charge of my private office. Access to me and my room was only available through this private office both literally and physically. I had my first experience of a regime which wished to enclose and nourish me with its own culture at the expense of being what I still was namely an MP with responsibilities to a constituency and in the House of Commons. The contest was joined early. My first encounter with answering parliamentary questions in the House of Commons on behalf of the Department was coming up soon. All my previous experience as a PPS and as a Whip told me that we should be looking for government success stories from the Department and 'planted' questions that would enable me to respond to these successes in an upbeat way on the Department's behalf. I put out an instruction accordingly. In no time at all a rather senior civil servant warned me off and indicated that this was a partisan activity and, as such, inappropriate. I backed off. I probably should not have done. He caused me enough doubt to stop me. There was no precedent in the L.C.D. I had no fellow House of Commons Minister in the Department to share this with nor any predecessor. Probably with hindsight I should have ignored his restraint. Anyway I think we all learned from this episode and what followed was a more relaxed approach to "good news" and a greater willingness to get it out.

The Lord Chancellor himself was not a stranger to me. During part of my time in the Whips Office I had the brief of Home Office and Legal Affairs Whip. Traditionally this had involved a heavy commitment to the conduct of the affairs of the Home Office. The second part of the title had been neglected. I had decided to do something about this and not only set up a modest meeting with the Attorney General, the Solicitor General and their Parliamentary Private Secretaries in the Attorney General's Chambers prior to Attorney General's questions on the floor of the House, but made it my business to get to know the Lord Chancellor and occasionally take small groups of Conservative M.P.s up to see him for general discussions, not least about Legal Aid. I had told the Lord Chancellor that if he wanted to regard me as the equivalent of his Parliamentary Private Secretary (PPS) and act as his eyes and ears in the House of Commons then I would be happy to do so. For reasons that have never been clear to me it seemed then to have been traditional that the Lord Chancellor did not have a P.P.S. Hence my offer. From the outset I admired Lord Mackay of Clashfern, his iron self-discipline, his great intelligence and his kindness. I have seldom, if ever, met a man of superior intellect. His ability to think problems through from first principles was awesome. Apart from anything else, here was a man with a first class honours degree in mathematics and a first class honours degree in law. Some would say that he was one of Margaret Thatcher's most inspired appointments. I think I would agree. Once she had decided that he was her man she would not have cared a jot that his years as a practitioner had been of Scottish rather than of English law.

My time in his Department was occupied, in part, by the conduct in the House of the Police and Magistrates Courts Bill which Michael Howard was advancing in respect of the Home Office parts of this Bill while I did the Lord Chancellor's Department parts. In particular we were reducing the number of magistrates courts committee areas. There were far too many (104) compared to the number of Police Authority areas (43), Probation Service areas (54) and Prosecuting Authority areas (now 42). This debate about the number of operational areas and their size was blessed with the ugly name 'Co-Terminosity'. In the end the arguments were good enough in management terms but fiefdoms were threatened and we certainly met organised resistance.

At the height of our difficulties with Magistrates re-organisation and London Magistrates jurisdictions in particular, I was invited to the Annual Dinner of the Middlesex Magistrates.

My officials had been told by them that no speech from me was required. Accordingly no text was provided for me.

When I got to the hotel I asked my hosts if this was still the case. They said "well just a word from you perhaps". Then, at table, I saw that I actually featured on the menu as a speaker.

Not only that but that I was to follow Gilbert Gray QC recently given the accolade of Speaker of the Year.

He was brilliant, of course, but in a handle-turning way, another audience, another entertainment.

I felt I had been set up. The celebrated Queen's Counsel and after dinner speaker was to be followed by the startled, unprepared, unpopular (with this audience) Junior Minister.

Well I could fight that. If they wanted twelve minutes 'rock and roll' from me then they could have it. I scribbled notes on the menu to speak from and gave them the works including a joke line, devised by me, which Gilbert Gray himself used at another function which I attended three months later. It was to the effect that I had missed many a good dinner (pause) through not being invited. At the later function he said that the Lord Chancellor had missed many a good dinner (pause) through not being invited.

I was much involved in the closure of County Courts. I was also very much involved in the affairs of the Public Record Office supervised by the

Chapter Twenty-three – The Lord Chancellor's Department

Keeper Mrs Sarah Tyack, a pleasantly efficient lady very much in-charge. Meanwhile the Chief Executive of the Legal Aid Board was Steve Orchard and the Chairman of that Board was an interesting and sagacious man by the name of John Pitts. Discussing the related subjects of quality control and value for money, he it was who said to me that "if a Ford would fail a specification as a Rolls Royce, remember that a Rolls Royce would fail a specification as a Ford".

Throughout my time at the Lord Chancellor's Department the head of the Land Registry (Chief Land Registrar and Chief Executive) was a splendid man by the name of John Manthorpe who had come up through the ranks of the Land Registry as a map man rather than as a lawyer, if I may put it like that. He always seemed to be in control of the affairs of the Land Registry which was, by then, developing into a very considerable success story. The Lord Chancellor's Department was well disposed to John Manthorpe not merely because he was a particularly agreeable man but also because his agency hardly created any problems for us at all.

These were my subject areas as I handled my brief in front of the House from the Dispatch Box, on behalf of the Department. Court closures were important, Magistrates' Courts jurisdictions were important but legal aid entitlement, or lack of it, remained, throughout my time, a matter of sometimes seething contention.

There was an unusual personal experience during my time in the Lord Chancellor's Department. It arose out of the fact that, apart from the Lord Chancellor himself, whose offices were anyway in the House of Lords, the Department had never before me had any other minister and the prospect of having one in their own midst in the Headquarters building created one small problem among many larger ones. As I may have already said, an office and an outer office had been carved out for me within the existing premises. Mine was a handsome room, I have to say. But there were no pictures whatever on the walls. I was to be allowed to chose my own prints which the Department would then have framed and hung for me. For this purpose several very large swatches of prints were brought to me. The selection at my disposal was so comprehensive as to be almost overwhelming. It was a task that could easily have been neglected for weeks as being of a really rather low priority. But I thought the appearance of the room was quite important and I made time selecting some five or six pictures. The room had one long wall with no windows. I thought it needed two large, confident pictures set symmetrically and hopefully hanging compatibly and congenially on the same wall. I chose a lake scene by Monet with a tree in the foreground and a characteristic Cezanne with hillsides in the background but which also had a lake in the foreground. The two pictures certainly looked well together and were commented upon, with approval, from time to time by some of my various visitors.

It was about six months later, maybe longer, that I found time to visit the Courtauld Collection in Somerset House.

There were, as there usually are, various rooms within the Gallery that led from one into another. As I entered the fourth such room I had quite a surprise. The original of the Cezanne and the original of the Monet were hanging next to each other on the same wall and in the same juxtaposition as I had the two prints in my office. I will not say that it did anything to the hairs on the back of my neck or that it 'took my breath away' as had happened on one occasion when first seeing a snow scene by Sisley in the Exhibition of Impressionist Art at the Royal Academy some years before. But it certainly was a remarkable experience.

Before I left the Lord Chancellor's Department for the DTI we were heading for the closing stages of the Family Law Bill and with it a number of ancillary recommendations of the Law Commission.

The ancillary provisions concerned property rights between 'partners' who were not married. Within the Lord Chancellor's Department I had argued consistently that ahead of a General Election that was going to be incredibly difficult to win, we did not need gratuitous battles with people who were otherwise on our side.

There was one personal achievement in the Lord Chancellor's Department which concerned a Private Members Bill initiated by Peter Thurnham (M.P. for Bolton North East). In this I had enormous help from a senior lawyer in the Lord Chancellor's Department called Jonathan Holbrook. It was all about the otherwise obscure subject of "privity of estate" and "privity of contract". I had identified as a law student long before that the law in this area of commercial leasing was extremely unfair. An original landlord of a commercial lease could hold the original tenant liable on the rental covenant against failure to pay the rent by a subsequent tenant. A retail newsagent, long retired, could find himself liable to pay rent in the event of default by a subsequent tenant, maybe two or three steps down the chain, even though he may have felt that he had parted with both interest and liability in respect of the property.

I met some unexpected resistance in helping Peter Thurnham with his Bill. It was as though our whips didn't want it. There is something of an aversion to Private Members' Bills in the Government Whips Office. Anyway we made a change in the Law which I think was thoroughly worth while.

Chapter Twenty-three – The Lord Chancellor's Department

From time to time in a politician's career one is asked "when did you ever make a difference?"

Perhaps this is my answer that in the closing stages of my time at the Lord Chancellor's Department I altered the Law on the liability of original tenants in commercial lettings.

My best memory of the Lord Chancellor's Department is of my gratitude to Magistrates. With whom I generally enjoyed working very much just as I had as a practising solicitor in my previous existence.

Chapter 24

The Department Of Trade And Industry

More Red Boxes

Joining the Department of Trade and Industry in November 1995 after serving in the Lord Chancellor's Department was like going aboard an aircraft carrier after having served on a minesweeper.

In terms of the comparative size, budget and range of responsibilities of these two Government Departments, that was the scale of the change.

The Department of Trade and Industry was in fact not one Department but five. It was the Department for Trade, the Department for Industry, the Department for Energy, the Department for Science and it was largely the Department for Employment notwithstanding that there was another Department of State known as the Department for Education and Employment.

My brief was to be Minister for Consumer Affairs; Competition Policy; Investigations; Companies Legislation and Regulations: the Companies House Agency; the Insolvency Service Agency; Industrial Relations; Industrial Tribunals; Redundancy Payments; Pay Issues and DTI Common Services. Like all DTI Ministers I was also to take a special interest in designated regions. In my case it was the West Midlands, of which I had special knowledge anyway, Merseyside and the North West. I suppose my parental background informed me tolerably well for the North West. Merseyside had been hived off from the North West at some relatively recent time in the past to form a separate region. I am in no doubt that ring-fencing Merseyside and isolating it as a region in its own right enabled it to qualify for Objective I status under the qualifying rules for entitlements under the European Structural Funds. Had Merseyside been aggregated with the rest of the, relatively more prosperous, North West, that categorisation would not have been achieved.

My regular regional visits were absorbing if not exactly exotic. The levels of partnership co-operation in the Liverpool area came as a very pleasant surprise in the post-Militant atmosphere that then prevailed.

It was in Manchester and subsequently from Edward Stobart (he of the Eddie Stobart trucks) that the Birmingham Northern Relief Road was as emphatically entreated in the North West as it was in the West Midlands.

On arrival at the Department I naturally first met the Head of my Private Office (Paul Hadley). I got to know that from the serial numbers of

Chapter Twenty-four – The Department Of Trade And Industry

the cars on the London Underground he could tell when and where they were made. I have to say that in his own way he was seriously loyal to me and I remain grateful to him.

I also had an important interview with the Department's Permanent Secretary, then Peter Gregson, who asked me all about my personal and financial affairs. I understood the necessity for this. It was vital that a DTI Minister with sensitive responsibilities should avoid any possible compromise or conflict of interest. Not only that but the Permanent Secretary, provided the Minister was utterly candid with him, could either assist the Minister with advice as to how to re-arrange his affairs or, if that was not readily possible, the Permanent Secretary and the Minister in question could create a cordon round a particular area of the Department's activity, preclude the Minister from ever entering that cordon by mutual agreement and then make that preclusion public knowledge. Furthermore, in my experience, if the Minister is utterly frank and co-operative in matters such as these then senior Civil Servants will strive mightily to keep the Minister out of trouble and keep a vigilant 'weather-eye' out for him as to any potential trouble coming over the horizon.

I knew all this and I told Peter Gregson all about my circumstances, including my dying mother's shareholding in Lonrho, the empire built up by 'Tiny' Rowland. We discussed this and I set in hand arrangements that when my mother did pass away (she died peacefully on Christmas Day of that year), the Lonrho shares should either go to my brother with a corresponding asset allocation to me or otherwise the Lonrho shareholding would be liquidated.

Peter Gregson consolidated our discussion by writing me a letter inviting me to confirm my circumstances. I replied comprehensively. Gregson would have put this exchange of letters on file, readily accessible in case of a problem. This was professional Civil Service thoroughness at its best. I was reassured by it and believed that I was responding in the same tenor.

As I write now I wonder what the corresponding interview might have been like between a more recent Permanent Secretary with Peter Mandelson on that man's becoming Secretary of State at the DTI. Events might suggest that he was not as candid as I was.

Shortly after joining the Department we had a weekend away at Chevening for a study session reviewing the Department's work. All the Ministers attended under Ian Lang who, as Secretary of State, had retained Michael Heseltine's title, President of the Board of Trade. Senior Civil Servants went with us and we had some stimulating outside speakers. At that stage I was still on a steep learning curve but I was beginning to enjoy it.

Gradually I got the hang of DTI Question Time in the House of Commons. Ian Lang decided which of his team would answer which questions. I could have two questions in succession or twenty minutes between questions allocated to me. How different at the Lord Chancellor's Department answering questions when I had to answer them all because there was only me to answer them.

Ian Lang was an able and unfussy Secretary of State. I was extremely impressed by his handling in the House of Commons of the Scott Report on 'Arms to Iraq'. The preparation for this must have been immense and only a man with a fine mind and ability to absorb detail in a short time and an unflappable temperament could have carried it off. But he did. It was one of the best parliamentary performances that I had witnessed in my time in the House.

Ian Lang was also a very good delegator though he used his own Private Office to keep close checks down the chain of command within the Department. I flatter myself to think that he actually thought that I was quite a 'safe pair of hands' for last-minute delegation. In the nature of his job as the Ministerial head of a very big and very important Department his settled schedule of engagement sometimes got ruptured at short notice by breaking news or events or developments. Thus it was that, as a junior Minister, I would sometimes arrive at my office in the D.T.I. in the morning with a settled programme of my own for which I had prepared the night before only to find my Private Secretary greeting me with a thick file and the news that I was due in a Cabinet Committee in twenty five minutes because the Secretary of State was on his way to the airport because such and such had happened overnight. In this sense, but only in this sense, I came to think that being a Junior Minister could actually be tougher than being a Senior Minister. I remember on one occasion abandoning my return arrangements to Solihull in favour of a short notice meeting of a Cabinet sub-committee to discuss the use of power stations to burn offending, or potentially offending material in the early stages of the B.S.E. crisis. I have to say that I did not enjoy these short-notice inter-departmental meetings and I was always made aware of the need to defend my Department from the expenditure consequences of decisions taken.

Back in the Department there were some very difficult questions for me on weights and measures, metrication and labelling and also with the De-Regulation Unit which was pretty hostile to most of the directives issuing from Brussels and, quite rightly, even more hostile to any hint that officials might be tempted to 'goldplate' them.

I have to say that this area of my work did give me one very pleasant interlude. Fortnum & Mason wanted a discussion with me about price labelling and related matters. I was happy to oblige them and received an

Chapter Twenty-four – The Department Of Trade And Industry

invitation to their famous store of which I had a conducted tour followed by a most agreeable lunch in their boardroom. Ministerial life is not all care and anxiety!

It was also part of my role to be a publicist for safety. We had campaigns on safety in the kitchen and safety in the garden. We also had a campaign on ladder safety. It really was quite remarkable how many people each year are injured or even killed by not using ladders sensibly.

More obviously potentially lethal were fireworks. In this I needed little encouraging. For me they had always been explosives. If any one person was hurt on firework night it was always one person too many for me. There is the welfare of frightened animals to be considered too. On 20 December 1996 I introduced Emergency Regulations to ban the sale of aerial shells and aerial maroons to the general public. Thereafter such fireworks could only be acquired or used by those properly in the business of operating firework displays. It had been quite a long haul to achieve this and I had met some opposition. But I will never concede that it was 'nannying'. These lethal so-called fireworks had been responsible in one or two instances for blowing peoples heads off in front of large numbers of spectators and even in front of their own children.

Two of the most interesting areas of my responsibility at the DTI were in respect of company law and investigations into suspicions of insider trading or events and transactions which might tend to suggest that certain persons had acted fraudulently or might otherwise be unsuitable to be a company director. These cases were fascinating and they appealed to the lawyer in me as well as the politician.

It led me to sign Public Interest Immunity Certificates from time to time. These had been notoriously discussed, explained and mis-explained during and since the Scott Enquiry into 'Arms for Iraq'.

Being of a cautious or even timid nature I took immense care with these P.I.I. Certificates. But I came to the conclusion that they were not as menacing as many would have us believe.

In effect they take the form of a communication by a Minister to a trial judge. They usually say that the Government, left to its own interests, would rather not have certain documents available to the trial for reasons such as the protection of persons who had (but might not otherwise have) given helpful evidence. But it is in the nature of such a Certificate that the final decision explicitly rests with the judge and if he or she thinks that the interests of justice can only properly be served by disclosure then the Government must and will accept that situation regardless of its own convenience. I never really saw anything wrong with that.

Meanwhile my role as Minister for Consumer Protection got me 'the bird' from a programme called 'Watchdog', an episode which actually engendered me more goodwill than damage. The consumer protection role also re-introduced me to working with the Citizens Advice Bureau and the National Consumer Council which I enjoyed.

But in the area of small business, not actually my brief within the Department but we all took an interest in small businesses, I was never really satisfied that the DTI truly understood small businesses. I never met a Civil Servant who had run one. I concede there may be a few somewhere. I merely say I never met one. Having myself employed every number of employees between one (my minimum) and twelve (my maximum), I felt I understood small businesses better than they did. This is not intended unduly critically. But I do think that the DTI's perception of the nature of businesses was only able to focus at businesses employing fifty and upwards. Significantly bigger than that and the DTI's perception was very good indeed. I just do not think they could get their sights down below fifty. Truly small businesses are "below the radar of the DTS. Meanwhile an analysis of employment in my own borough of Solihull shows that 86.1 per cent of all businesses, measured by size, actually have 24 employees or less. This is quite a large proportion of the economy to be of out of sight of the Department of Trade and Industry!

After Paul Hadley I had Dawn Parr as the Head of my Private Office. Of the five Heads of Private Office that I had had as a Departmental Minister (three at the Lord Chancellor's Department and two at the DTI) she was quite the best and we were both still in post, working together very happily, at least as far as I am concerned, when the 1997 Election drew near. When it was called I think I knew that we would lose. A short while into the campaign I cleared my desk.

Chapter 25

An Interlude On Islands

'Oh, it's a snug little island! A right little, tight little island.'
The Snug Island by Thomas John Dibdin

I put my binoculars on Benbecula from Skye. It was the first time I had had a prospect of the Outer Hebrides. It also enabled me to get Bonnie Prince Charlie's famous boat trip the right way round. Of course he was not outbound to Skye he was inbound from Benbecula. The distance between the mainland and Skye hardly merited an heroic Boat Song. It was a short ferry journey when I was there and it now has a controversial toll bridge.

But I determined that I would go to see the Outer Hebrides which I did a year later. I took a plane from Glasgow which landed on the beach at Barra, a novel experience. There was a hire car waiting for me with its ignition key in the exhaust pipe. I managed to get to see all six main islands of which the other five are South Uist, Benebecula, North Uist, Harris and Lewis. Harris and Lewis are connected to each other, but only just, or so it seems. In fact they have a strange boundary.

The following year I visited Orkney and The Shetlands.

The Outer Hebrides have a Gaelic feel about them. Orkney and Shetland are more Nordic. They are all very beautiful.

I do not know when I first became conscious of my affinity for islands. It may have been in one of those early Sennen Cove holidays when we flew from a grass airfield at St Just to St Mary's in the Scilly Isles.

Otherwise it may have been when on a school boy trip with Eversfield to Largs in Ayrshire we took boat trips on the steamer called 'Duchess of Fife' to Millport on Great Cumbrae Island and Rothesay on the Isle of Bute and Brodick on the Isle of Arran. On Arran there is a famous mountain called Goatfell of 2867 feet. A famous murder took place there.

During these island crossings in the Firth of Clyde the Royal Navy was at anchor, deployed in formation, ready for inspection. It was an awesome and impressive display of power to a twelve year old.

Islands are axiomatically self-contained. They exist as they are, self-evidently unconnected and, as such, have an individual character and atmosphere and culture too, if they are inhabited.

The human culture of Bermuda, for instance, on the one hand and of the incomparably larger Cuba on the other could not be more different.

Bermuda is rich, Cuba, which has the greater potential to be so, is not. Visiting Cuba I was subjected to some of the most insistent begging I have ever encountered. It is the human culture, the politics, which has produced this sharp disparity.

Physical differences can be quite marked as well. In the Eastern Caribbean I visited Anguilla, Montserrat, Antigua and St Lucia. Montserrat is volcanic as we all now know well enough. It was only smoking when I was there. St Lucia is volcanic too but Antigua and Anguilla are really coral islands and much flatter and, to my eye, less verdant than their volcanic neighbours.

Perhaps the most impressive volcanic island which is quite readily attainable from home is Madeira where I have had a number of holidays. It rises to six thousand feet out of the Atlantic and it is the nearest 'piece of paradise', as far as I am concerned.

Whilst Madeira is Portugese, the nearby Canary Islands are, of course, Spanish but the rocks and flora do not know that, nor do they need to. Tenerife is very familiar to many British holiday makers and Lanzarote to quite a few as well but the interior of Gran Canaria, in my opinion, rivals Madeira and it is the Canary Island to which I might be most inclined to return.

I have a special affection for Gibraltar which is a political island if not a physical one though it is not difficult to imagine that in geological time it might have been periodically unconnected from the Spanish mainland, so relatively tenuous may have been the isthmus that connects it now.

Majorca is an intrinsically beautiful island and I have enjoyed myself on holiday there and once even went to Majorca for lunch! But I found Minorca more satisfying not least for its neolithic antiquities, its 'monumentos megaliticos'.

The antiquities of Rhodes are, in some instances, slightly puzzling and disappointing to the extent that they were 'improved' by the occupying Italians during the Second World War. A ruin should be a ruin, preserved and cared for certainly but not put back together again with whatever good intention by those who come later.

I heard just a little of the same criticism of Knossos on Crete but Knossos worked alright for me as did the whole of Crete which has a hardness that might translate into Spanish as Estremadura.

Paros and Naxos in the Aegean have a personal compulsion for me because it was from Naxos to Paros that I served as boatman, feeder and keeper of the log to Dr Chris Stockdale during his epic ten hour swim between the two islands which nobody had ever accomplished before.

Chapter Twenty-five – An Interlude On Islands

Chris Stockdale is a legend of marathon swimming, he has swum the Channel three times but far more besides, and he has raised huge sums of money for charity in the process. His supporters, including me, were the house guests of John Polyzoides at his splendid villa on Paros to which he has subsequently retired. (He it was, many years before, whose careful advice had brought my cricket career to a painless conclusion).

Sicily is magnificent in its antiquities not least at Syracuse but it is very heavily populated by I think, five million people. The motor car traffic can be oppressive on Sicily but it has some breath-taking highway engineering as certain of the principal roads, particularly in the east, seem to be on viaducts or in tunnels all the way. Say what you like about the Italians but they are defiant engineers.

Before my trip to Hong Kong I tried to visualise what it would be like and to find a way of turning that into words. The best I could do was a cross between Gibraltar and Manhattan. As a matter of fact it turned out not be too far different from that idea except it was bigger and, of course, absolutely seething with enterprise of which gambling seemed to be an habitual extension. They pay for the welfare budget out of a tax on horse racing. Which either means that proportionately there are not many people on welfare or, just as likely, betting on horses is prodigious. I suspect both may be true.

Mentioning Manhattan, which is indeed an island, is to speak of one of the most remarkable human settlements in the world. It has in common with Hong Kong a deeply stable geology which permits very high buildings in both places. Apart from its many fascinations, there was a thing which puzzled me about Manhattan. How could some of the most valuable real estate in the world be at close quarters with dereliction. Not much dereliction, I allow, but a noticeable amount. I would have thought that in a free market, and America is just that or nowhere is, the derelict sites would have been keenly competed for at whatever price prevailed.

Closer to home, I visited the Isle of Man in my student days to watch the TT motor cycle racing there and unfortunately saw not a lot else of that interesting island with its unique relationship to the United Kingdom.

Much more recently I was very pleasantly surprise by Anglesey which, and I will not abuse the word, is very pretty and on a very comfortable scale.

I think one could say the same, maybe slightly more so, for the Isle of Wight which contains within itself an extraordinary environmental variety. The built environment is impressive too, not least Osborne House, much loved by Queen Victoria.

Please Stay To The Adjournment

If the Scillies were the first islands that I went to, then the Channel Islands were the next. Initially I camped on Jersey with its wonderful beaches, its martello towers and its reminders of World War II. Also the buses had my initials on them JMT for Jersey Motor Transport.

Many years later I was to go to Guernsey which I think I prefer and took a boat and walked round its little brother Herm.

Mauritius, in the Indian Ocean, was the venue of an Anglo-Mauritian trade fair when I was at the DTI and it was my good fortune to be the British Minister sent out for the occasion. It was an eight-day idyll. Mauritius has beaches the like of which I had only seen in the creative photography of holiday brochures and the magazine sections of Sunday newspapers. There were amazing volcanic skylines too, dramatically jagged against the sunset. [1]

Government responsibility also took me on another occasion to the Island of St Helena in the South Atlantic, the final home of Napoleon as a British captive. To this day St Helena has no air strip and is accessible only by the boat which visits the Island via the Canaries and Ascension Island (onwards to Cape Town) eight times a year. I flew from Brize Norton in Oxfordshire with the RAF and landed at Wideawake airfield on Ascension Island, which was a remarkable place in itself, with some hours to spare before intercepting the southbound mail boat. My flight had been timed, of course, to coincide with the boat's call at Ascension.

The south-bound boat journey to St Helena and, indeed, subsequently onward to Cape Town was a life time experience. We had a total sea scape with sightings of whales and flying fish and we were tracked for hours by an albatross.

First sightings of St Helena left one in no doubt as to what a formidable fortress it could be. It rises out of the South Atlantic like a molar tooth. It has no harbour that one could describe as such. It is necessary for an approaching vessel to drop anchor and for passengers like myself to go ashore in a launch from which it is necessary to grab the handrails of the gangway at the quay side from the deck of the launch even as it rises and falls on the swell.

I had gone to St Helena on behalf of the Government during my time in the Whips Office. Either there were no Foreign Office Ministers available or else it was considered an insufficiently important mission for one of them and therefore appropriate to a Whip. Be that as it may, it was my profound

---

1. *The politically interesting thing about the Anglo-Mauritian trade fair was that three of the main exhibitors were Land Rover (selling Discoveries to the Mauritian police), Solihull College seeking an education contract with the island's authorities and Severn Trent Water also successfully pursuing a drainage contract. All three, like me, were from Solihull but had to be in the Indian Ocean to be under one roof!*

Chapter Twenty-five – An Interlude On Islands

good fortune. A very full eight day programme awaited me of which the two most important were the Official Opening of the Prince Andrew School and the visit, with locally elected councillors, to the site of a possible air strip.

As to the second of these, there is a touching by-line. The councillors, when they could bring themselves to tell me, actually didn't really want an air strip. They really wanted more frequent connections by boat to their relatives on Ascension.

I think I could have written a whole chapter, if not a book, about St Helena, but that is not my purpose. I will content myself with saying, as I thought of it at the time, that St Helena is a small island with a huge landscape. As I continued my memorable voyage to Cape Town, I savoured the departing view of St Helena, the view Napoleon never had.

Of all these islands it is difficult to think in terms of favouritism or whether to measure them against the test of whether I would like to go back. Tresco was perhaps the prettiest and most peaceful, Madeira continues to be a regular holiday venue for me, St Helena remains the great adventure, Seaforth Loch, where Harris meets Lewis was perhaps the greatest splendour and I could have spent more time on the beaches of Mauritius.

I end on Islay in the Inner Hebrides, Easter 2002, trapped in the Bunnahabhain ('boon-a-harven') distillery by an articulated lorry slewed across the only, single-tracked, road in and out of it and which was bogged down to its axles in the peat on either side of the road. Its intended mission had been to deliver some casks to the distillery. Meanwhile I had gone to the distillery, for a handsomely conducted tourist visit, in my own car, which was, by now, marooned on the far side of this obstruction.

It was a Bank Holiday and it took several hours for the distillery manager to get a huge and immensely powerful tractor from a local quarry. This monster eventually squared up the lorry, thereby re-opening the road. I was forced to spend the intervening time at the distillery watching the late afternoon sun go down on the Sound of Islay, fortified only by free samples.

Afterwards I was able to return to the excellent Machrie Hotel where I was staying. My companion of that Easter holiday drove us home in my car. We got there in good time for dinner. Only my closest friends will understand that I had to draw down on all my experience and resolution to cope with this crisis. Trapped on an island. Confined in a distillery.

Chapter 26

The Night Of 1997

Firestorm

It had been a ghastly election and a long one too. John Major had run to his last option in naming May 1st 1997 as Polling Day and we took a five week run at it. The effort had been to try to tell the British electorate how strong the economy was by virtue of our stewardship. I believe our record on privatisation (getting large areas of the economy out from under the Treasury and incidentally ending "political strikes") coupled with de-regulation, improved industrial relations, wider share ownership and sound fiscal policy had rendered the general economic situation arguably better than it had ever been. However, for at least the first fortnight, our message was seldom better than third slot on the national news. We were drowned out, not least, by the developments at Tatton. Neil Hamilton was in deep trouble in that otherwise safe Conservative seat and the developing story was that one after the other the Liberal Democrat and Labour candidates withdrew in favour of Martin Bell the popular war correspondent with the trademark white suit. We also had the bizarre rompings of Piers Merchant in Beckenham. All this was more entertaining than economics, bad for our image and diverting from our message.

In Solihull itself it was quite my worst Election. The three-year saga of uncertainty concerning Solihull hospital, had understandably taken its toll and the Save Solihull Hospital campaign wanted a final political squeeze on the candidates at a political meeting which they set up for the purpose. When that meeting assembled in Shirley, it got off to a surreal start. In addition to the three main candidates, Conservative, Lib Dem and Labour, who had committed themselves to participating, there appeared the Pro-Life candidate and the Referendum candidate who insisted with some justice that they were entitled to be part of the meeting as well. This was undesired and unintended by the organisers. A debate took place on whether all the candidates should take part which was at once principled and anarchic with contending claims and counter-claims for fair play, and equal treatment on the one hand and the maintenance of the original purpose of the meeting on the other. The meeting was also weakly chaired by the editor of one of the two local newspapers who had been chosen for the merit of his neutrality. In fairness to him he certainly lived up to that credential and did his best. It

Chapter Twenty-six – The Night Of 1997

would in any event have been a desperately difficult meeting for anyone to chair with authority. But as a forum intended to press the candidates on the subject of the hospital, it had lost its edge and never recovered. All five candidates insisted on answering every question. Unsurprisingly the least experienced gave the longest answers.

There was another shared platform meeting for all the candidates, organised by the Churches. This is one I always do. And finally another, on eve of poll, at the Sixth Form College which proved to be lively and interesting and where, in a subsequent ballot of those attending I learnt that I had come second to the Labour candidate. Even in a good year that would probably have been par for the course. The meeting was also interesting in that, not for the first time, the Referendum candidate Mike Nattrass told the audience quite casually that I would be the winner in the Solihull constituency.

We went to the count.

I had delayed my own arrival to pick up from television as much as I could of whatever trend was emerging from other declarations. A swing against us of 10% or more appeared to be the pattern. At the count it was soon clear that I was winning with a reduced majority. In Solihull, maybe elsewhere too, once the total vote has been established, the ballot papers favouring each of the individual candidates (there were five of us) are separated, counted into bundles of twenty-five then into bundles of one hundred and finally aggregated into bundles of one thousand. Once verified they are then taken to a vast horizontal wooden frame, compartmentalised or pigeon-holed to accommodate these bundles of one thousand votes in a way that allows an obvious visual linear assessment of each candidates's score. It is a sort of moving bar chart. In the event I had a 10.3% swing against me, which proved to be slightly lower than the national average.

I subsequently learnt that after a hundred declarations on that fateful night there was only one Conservative MP. It was me. Cecil Parkinson, with the unenviable task of being the Conservative spokesman on one of the two channels of TV coverage greeted my result by saying "well now we have a leader!". About thirty five minutes later when there was a second Conservative MP returned, he developed this by saying "well now we have a contest!".

We retired for consoling drinks at Pauline Blow's home and watched the full extent of the defeat.

At one stage during that night I had a conversation alone with Brenda Young who had been Chairman of the Association for the last three years and had been my agent during the election too, perhaps the best I ever had. She asked me what was the most useful thing that I thought I could do for the Party now we were so reduced and so obviously in opposition. I told her that the best thing that could happen to me would be to be invited back into the Conservative Whips Office. There I felt I could provide a measure of experience and guidance amid the initial demoralisation but hopefully, in due time, the beginnings of recovery.

Chapter 27

A New Start

"Smiling at Grief"

When we got back to the House of Commons after the Election it was of course to a completely changed political landscape. There were obvious things like absent friends and sitting on the Opposition side of the Chamber, on the Speaker's left. There were obvious conversations between surviving Conservative MPs on the lines "how much damage did UKIP or the Referendum Party do in your constituency?" or rueful note taken of those seats where such an intervention, on the face of it, had cost a colleague his or her seat.

There was a more or less undignified scramble for rooms especially among those of us who had been ministers. I got down very early for this purpose and secured for myself a decent room, not too ambitious. There was a brand new intake of approximately forty new Conservative MPs whom I subsequently came to regard as the most talented intake in my time. By contrast the New Labour intake was, of course, huge, unaware of the customs of the place, triumphalist and seemingly determined, every time they roughly got the hang of some established custom or practice, to make darn sure they would change it. Or so it seemed.

Many of them had been councillors and continued to behave as councillors. Early on there were incidents of clapping by way of applause in the Chamber. Fortunately Madam Speaker Boothroyd gave early indications of defending the traditions of the House of Commons and, my word, a strong Speaker was needed in these new circumstances. She *was* a strong speaker.

Only after a passage of quite a lot more time did the new Labour intake begin to realise that, aside from being opponents, we were also colleagues in the sense of belonging to the same institution. Not for the first time, I suspect, the House of Commons as an institution began to assert itself over its members. I suppose the process was never entirely complete in that, as I write, two and half years into that parliament, the Government continues, on not infrequent occasions to treat the House of Commons too casually as it is from time to time splendidly reminded by Tony Benn. I paraphrase: "Our long struggle has been between King and Parliament but what do you do when the King is in 10 Downing Street?"

However in the earliest stages of our return John Major announced that he would stand down from the leadership of the Conservative Party. The wounded residue of Conservative MPs now divided into six camps, soon reduced to five, to fight a civil war for the leadership against a background of critical mood music from some Conservative Associations and Area Organisations who believed that it was Conservative MPs, by their behaviour, who had contributed most to the election defeat and who had made it bitterly difficult for the party volunteer workers on the ground, themselves blameless, who had fought the election on the doorsteps in the face of an unprecedentedly hostile reception. The voluntary party had reason to be demoralised and angry. Someone or something was to blame and it certainly wasn't them. I was personally unsympathetic to those Conservative MPs who at various meetings in Westminster and up and down the country were not prepared to sit quietly and absorb the flak while the volunteers who had worked to put them where they were said what they felt and got it off their chests.

The voluntary party wanted to have a hand in the election of the new leader too. They were to get a series of straw polls, which they were to take seriously. They would get much more later.

After Stephen Dorrell had dropped out of the leadership contest, which he did in a seemly way after assessing that he did not have enough support, there remained five candidates. There was the moderate, experienced Euro-leaning Kenneth Clarke. In the country at large he was the candidate easily best known and, almost certainly, best liked. Michael Howard represented a serious candidate from the right, an intelligent, incisive debater carrying with him the recent and deserved reputation as a no-nonsense Home Secretary. I chaired his Birmingham campaign meeting. Peter Lilley came from about the same part of the spectrum but seemed to many to have a rather less focused image and a rather less clear-cut platform, although the one may have coloured the other. John Redwood, (at a personal level, I like him) who had challenged John Major in the 'leadership assertion' election of July 1995 was far from unknown. He seemed to have a clear-cut policy on everything, almost a caricature of a right-wing candidacy and an identifiable group of very close adherents whose very nature guaranteed that a more-or-less equal number of others would never vote for him. The last candidate was William Hague. At first it was rumoured that he had been likely to be a sort of designated number two in the Howard campaign. What the Americans might call a running mate. But the Hague campaign emerged in its own right and it was never to be shaken.

On personal grounds and loyalty grounds I wanted to support Clarke but his views on Europe were not mine and I felt that if he won and tried to make his own policies on Europe into the party line then we should be back

Chapter Twenty-seven – A New Start

into the hopeless struggles about Europe that had characterised the later Major years. I made my view known to him in something like those terms.

In the first ballot I supported Michael Howard but, in the event, he and Peter Lilley got the two lowest scores of votes out of the five candidates. They jointly withdrew.

Clarke was in the lead, Hague second and Redwood third.

The second ballot did not alter this order but it did not secure a decisive lead for Clarke. It did compel the withdrawal of Redwood who then surprised everyone by lining up with Clarke. My own view is that a number of the voters (Conservative MPs) were uneasy about this and, as the arithmetic undoubtedly shows, Redwood certainly did not take all his followers with him.

Hague won.

Hague then began to make his Shadow appointments. I was not included. I was neither aggrieved nor surprised but I was determined to give him my unswerving support, which I think I can fairly say that I did.

So it was that I had to look at my own position. It was pretty much in my own hands now either to struggle to get something or simply to settle for nothing. That did not take long to decide. The most that a back-bencher could get was a vice-chairmanship of one of our so called back bench committees. The chairmanship of those committees went, ex-officio, to the shadow cabinet member, appointed by Hague, to that area of responsibility. Accordingly I stood for election to the vice chairmanship first of the Trade and Industry Committee and then of the Legal Affairs Committee. These reflected my areas of ministerial experience. I won both, which was encouraging. Rather out of curiosity, I also accepted one of our places on the Council of Europe. This indirectly reflected my earlier experience in the European Parliament.

So I had carved out for myself a reasonable and relevant range of things to do and worked at them up to the Summer Recess at the end of July.

After the holiday and party conference season the House resumed in October for what is commonly called 'the carry over session' prior to Prorogation and the State Opening and a new Queen's Speech early in November.

Then, out of the blue, on the morning of Monday 3 November 1997. I received a phone call from the Conservative Chief Whips secretary to ask if I would be ready to take a call from the Chief himself, James Arbuthnot. This was interesting and I took the call with curiosity, at least. He said he would like me to re-join the Whips office. I accepted almost before he had finished asking me. I did go on to say that I would be slightly uncomfortable at re-joining our Whips office as the Junior Whip. The Conservative Whips office, in Government or Opposition, has a conscious regime of seniority. He put me at my ease by saying that he thought that was an entirely appropriate consideration and that I would be re-joining the office with rank of number four, that is to say immediately below the Chief, the Deputy Chief Whip and the Pairing Whip. That was gratifying and appreciated by me. I asked him what was to be the time of that day's Whips Office meeting. He said 2.30pm. It was mid morning and I was in Solihull. I went to the station, caught the train and was in my place at the meeting at 2.30pm.

I was back in "the Office" which was where, six months before, in the early hours of May 2nd, I had told Brenda Young that I thought I could be of most use.

Chapter 28

A Whip Again

"Managing Chaos"

After James Arbuthnot had rung me on the morning of Monday 3 November 1997, which call I had taken in my office in Solihull, my appointment to the Conservative Whips Office, ranked fourth in seniority, was confirmed by William Hague during Tuesday 4 November.

I had, in the meantime, attended my first Whips Office meeting on the Monday afternoon.

I liked the people that I found around me. The Whips Office is usually like that anyway and, as ever in such circumstances, I felt entitled to believe privately that they had chosen me because they wanted me, I felt I could make a contribution and that I would fit in.

In Opposition we were running on a Whips complement of ten, from the Chief Whip to the Junior Whip. This contrasted with my experience of fourteen Whips when we were in Government. I think this current Labour Government is running on a complement of sixteen Whips.

Since these reflections are now rather closer to the present day, the reader may be assured that I will not further drop my guard in relation to matters only known to me because of my membership of "the Office".

I will however record a glimpse into the experience of whipping two particular Bills as the Conservative Whip appointed to the relevant Standing Committees.

The first of these was the National Minimum Wage Bill. It was a substantial Bill and properly susceptible to a great deal of scrutiny and argument.

The reader will be aware that after the Second Reading of a Bill on the floor of the House of Commons, which is the occasion for general debate about the issues involved, the Bill then passes to a committee selected for the purpose for detailed, line by line, examination and debate. The committee sits, unsurprisingly, in a Committee Room on the main committee corridor of the House of Commons up on the first floor. These committee deliberations, usually held on Tuesdays and Thursdays, in morning, afternoon and evening sessions for as long as the job lasts or, in co-operative 'peace time conditions', in conformity with an approximate timetable worked out between the Government Whip and the Opposition Whip with the concurrence of minor parties wherever possible.

On this Committee there were six Conservatives. The balance of representation on the Committee is worked out in accordance with a formula reflecting the composition of the House of Commons itself. The presence of six Conservatives indicates to anyone familiar with the workings of that Parliament that it was a large committee. Indeed there were seventeen Labour members, including the Ministers having conduct of the Bill, there were two Liberal Democrat members and one Scottish National Party member, a Committee of twenty six members plus a Chairman.

Our team was led by Tim Boswell as the Shadow Minister and, with me as the Whip, the other four Conservative members were Andrew Lansley, John Bercow, Philip Hammond and Damian Green.

It would be entirely fair to say that the Bill was 'front-end-loaded', that is to say all its most serious, disputable and debatable provisions were in its early clauses.

This gave us the beginnings of a quite serious misunderstanding, which was to have a gruelling consequence.

I have no doubt that Clive Betts, the Government Whip on the committee, was under some pressure from the Government Whips Office to make some progress. That would not be unusual.

Meanwhile, as the debates wore on and the committee days went by we were still grinding away on the earliest of the early and most consequential clauses.

I thought that he and I had a timetable agreement and I continued to try to reassure him that although not much progress was being made we would nonetheless complete the scrutiny by a finishing date for the committee stage which ought to be acceptable to the Government. After all we would be devoting much less time to later clauses.

Wrongly, in my opinion, I think he had either begun to doubt our good faith or his superiors had.

By now this had ceased to be a struggle about scrutiny of this Bill. It had become more fundamental than that. It had become a trial of strength.

It was for us about the Government's power, as the Executive, to overwhelm the Committee and to that extent Parliament itself.

In any event the portents of all night sitting in committee began to appear and Clive Betts hinted the same. The Government's idea would be that by helping themselves to the relative eternity of an all night sitting or by exhausting us, or both, they would achieve great swathes of clauses hastening the end of the deliberations. After all their side did not have to participate in any of the debates on any of the clauses or any of the amendments which we had put down beyond brief ministerial

Chapter Twenty-eight – A Whip Again

introductions or replies. Nor did they. Nor did any of their back benchers join in any more than ours would have done if roles had been reversed. In short it was absolutely down to us either to keep the debates going or to begin desperately to concede ground like a losing tug of war team, and even, horror of horrors, get into open country beyond the clauses where we had managed, working ahead of the progress of the committee, to have our own amendments tabled and in place giving us the fertility of having something to talk about!

The all night session duly came on Tuesday, January 27th 1998 and we took the strain as the clock passed ten o'clock heading for midnight and the early hours.

I have to say that Tim Boswell, in the lead for us, was absolutely magnificent. It was a genuine tour de force. His knowledge of the subject matter and his ability to talk about each clause and each amendment comprehensively and at length gave a magnificent example to our four new back benchers. Lansley, Bercow, Hammond and Green were part of the new intake of which I have expressed my admiration elsewhere. This was the Conservative intake that, finding little by way of instruction or even instructors among their elder brethren upon their arrival, had simply broken down the doors of the armoury, helped themselves to rifles and started shooting.

Given the example of Tim Boswell each one of them responded amazingly and they relayed as a team, intervened on each other to give the one who was speaking pause for breath and sustained debate after debate comprehensively. Such was our ability to keep debates going, line by line, that the Labour Whip repeatedly had to resort to the closure to end debates which we could have maintained for longer. In this, of course, he had a difficulty in that the Chair will only entertain a closure motion if its occupant is satisfied that all reasonable arguments have already been heard. This is hazardous for a Government Whip because if the Chair is not so satisfied then the closure is not allowed, and an encouraged opposition can press on in the knowledge that the Government Whip will have to let quite a long time go by without risking the same tactic again.

As Tuesday night went into Wednesday morning and ultimately daylight came we knew that the Committee could not proceed beyond lunchtime that is to say one o'clock on the following day. We made it to one o'clock and the Government's progress was still only limited. They tried to announce a triumph in the name of the Labour back benchers on the Committee and in the name of the minimum wage. But it was not their triumph it was ours and I believe we had shaken them.

Please Stay To The Adjournment

The Committee next met on the Thursday of the same week and had a morning session, as usual, an afternoon session and, as ever, we went into the evening after dinner. Pretty soon it was clear that they were going to take us through the night again. The best indicators that this is going to happen are House of Commons staff, not least a skeleton catering staff who are put on readiness to go through the night themselves. And so we did it again and by six o'clock on what was by then Friday morning January 30th, with their Ministers needing to attend events in the provinces, the Government pulled stumps.

They had taken us through the night again and even as we debated we were drafting forward amendments as well. We continued to provide ourselves with material for argument ahead and beyond the point of progress.

They had not broken us and they had not made the sort of progress that they wanted to either.

This was the week when I went to bed on Monday night, Wednesday night and Friday night. It was tough going but I enjoyed it when it was done. It was good to know that one could still do it. It was good to know that the Conservatives that I served with on that committee were as resolute as they were. At one stage, during the second night, I offered them a roster so that each in turn could take a break. We were all sat together at a table in the tea room during a brief adjournment. None of them replied so I repeated the question. Again no reply. Then I said "do I take it that you all want to see this through together?" They nodded their assent. I tried not to show it but I was quite choked by this display of determination.

Pretty soon afterwards overtures for talks were received by us from the Government's side and we sat down in a friendly atmosphere and agreed a timetable which was honoured to the completion of the committee stage of the Bill.

At about this time Caroline Spelman came into the Office, my next door neighbour from the Meriden half of Solihull. She was to be an excellent and assiduous Whip, typical of all the things she did.

Her workload in the Office was very considerable and, in consequence, I became the Whip responsible for the Committee stage of another critical Bill, the Greater London Authority Bill, on which Peter Brooke played such a significant part. Ken Livingstone was also a member of the Committee. Throughout I expected he would stand as a candidate for Mayor of London. As I write now this has become a reality. It has become a substantial embarrassment for Labour.

I enjoyed my return to the Conservative Whips Office in opposition which lasted from November 1997 until 11th November 1999 when I

Chapter Twenty-eight – A Whip Again

received a phone call from our Chief Whip, James Arbuthnot, to ring William Hague, our Leader, who was, incidentally, utterly supported by me. He asked me to leave the Whips Office and become a Northern Ireland spokesman and I readily accepted.

So, in the idiom of the Whips Office which had always conceived there to be an imaginary 'Escape Committee', I had escaped twice. This was unusual.

Chapter 29

Northern Ireland

"No country in the world is less fitted for a conflict with terrorists than Great Britain, not because of our weakness and cowardice, but because of our restraint and our virtues". Winston S Churchill

When I first became a parliamentary candidate (in 1972, in Dudley East) it became clear to me that I needed a 'position to take' on the then present state of the troubles in Northern Ireland. In a constituency like Dudley East, it was also necessary to be possessed of a 'position to take' on Enoch Powell!. In the part of the world where I was then a candidate, where you stood on Enoch, was, regrettable as it may seem with hindsight, a public issue. I dealt with that in one way. Simply by going to see him. In an undeserved debating advantage, I was always able to say, at public meetings, 'when I went to see Mr Powell recently and raised this with him he said to me ....'. This may have been a contrivance. It almost certainly was. But it was not untruthful. Never was any member of my audience or any political opponent entitled to the same preference. I had the edge. It may not have been any more than a debating technique but I was never out-faced, I had the upper hand in those matters where a personality had became an issue.

In fact, Enoch's position had become more poignant by the time of the October 1974 Election because he stood in that Election, my second, as an Ulster Unionist.

It occurred to me that no amount of immersion in the then current issues in Northern Ireland would really make sense without a proper attempt to study the history of Ireland in general and the history of Partition, in particular. The first of these would need to go back at least three hundred years. The second at least back to Gladstone and the Irish Party and the Home Rule question as it was seen in Britain in the late nineteenth century and especially in the 1880s.

It was obvious to me that if Gladstone had succeeded the whole history of relations between Britain and Ireland would have taken a different course. But Gladstone did not succeed.

As a by-product of his Home Rule endeavours, however, and in particular in consequence of his need to do something about the parliamentary tactics of the Irish Party, Gladstone did achieve something

Chapter Twenty-nine – Northern Ireland

else. He devised some "brakes" that could be applied to proceedings in the House of Commons. Until that time consideration of business in the House could last as long as any determined group of people wanted it to. The debate would go on until the last person had said his last word. Incidentally the rules of procedure of the House of Lords are still like that. But in their Lordships House, in modern times, an exploitation of that state of affairs is virtually unthinkable.

Gladstone changed the rules for the House of Commons by introducing, not least, the Ten O'clock Rule which, if unsuspended, terminated business each day at that hour. He also introduced the Closure. That is to say a motion "that the question be now put". Such a motion, having been moved, always provided the Speaker is satisfied that there has been adequate argument, is not itself debatable. It must be voted on immediately. If there is a majority in favour the debate is closed and a further and immediate division must follow on the substantive question on which debate had been closed.

Finally he introduced a rule for a quorum of the House under which a Member present, doubting the existence of the quorum, could call upon the Speaker to test the question with a division.

By all these techniques Gladstone sought to prevent a group of members, speaking and resting in relays, from sustaining a sitting indefinitely.

After the turn of the century the Unionists from Ulster, notably Craig and Carson began a more aggressive campaign for the continued union of some part of the north of Ireland, preferably all of Ulster whatever proposals might still be under consideration for the South.

The First World War postponed an attempted settlement of all these angry and unresolved issues but not without the Easter Rising of 1916.

After the Armistice of 1918 further attempts were made to seek a resolution and dangerous negotiations began to lay the ground for the Partition of Ireland into an independent Republic in the south, sometimes referred to as the Free State and a preservation within the United Kingdom of some portion of the north.

But here was a real difficulty. That province of Ireland known as Ulster actually contained nine counties. Of these only four could be said to be predominantly unionist. The preservation within the United Kingdom of a mere four counties was considered a scarcely viable proposition. Furthermore it would hardly entitle such a territory to claim the name of Ulster. The final compromise, which, like most such comprises, hardly pleased anyone was that six counties would remain in the United Kingdom. The four obvious ones: Antrim, Armagh, Down and Derry plus Fermanagh and Tyrone. The last two barely, if at all, carrying Unionist credentials or aspirations. Meanwhile Donegal, Cavan and Monaghan, whilst remaining in Ulster, were included in the Republic of Ireland.

Whatever the feelings about the out-turn in the north, there were severe internal enmities in the south that led to civil war with the chief protagonists being Michael Collins and Eamon de Valera.

The overall situation smouldered through recession and until another World War diverted almost everyone's attention.

Post war, the Unionists invariably dominated Stormont but there was an awareness, still years from being a general British awareness, of discrimination in jobs and housing, in particular.

Mainland "troubles" resumed, not least with bombings in Coventry in the 1950's.

The eventual commitment of a British military presence in Northern Ireland in August 1969 to reinforce conventional policing began to raise public consciousness that something serious had to be done and that the terrorist activities of the IRA were not some kind of lingering romanticism for a United Ireland but intolerable criminal atrocities.

Various initiatives such as Sunningdale, the efforts of John Major's government and, most recently, the Good Friday or Belfast Agreement have attempted to achieve both a peace process and a "Power-sharing Executive" spawned from a devolved elected Assembly.

The guiding principle always being that the communities of Northern Ireland should be jointly confronted with the need to address their own problems, govern their own affairs and make some hard decisions within the context of a democratic political framework.

The need for reciprocity between the various intransigent, mistrustful, vengeful, wounded or simply demoralised and frightened communities lay at the heart of these processes. It was soon seen to be extremely fragile as the principal, often less that full-hearted, participants protested that it was they who were being called upon to make all the sacrifices without getting anything adequate in return. I confess to being a Unionist sympathiser in this and believe the greatest mistake was the wholesale release of terrorist prisoners without any apparent de-commissioning of terrorist weaponry whatsoever.

As I write (2003) I am not optimistic about the future of Northern Ireland. The government were mistaken, in my view, in the dissolution of the Stormont institutions last year as evidence emerged as to what I can only call espionage by Sinn Fein. Sinn Fein alone should have been disqualified. Now normalising elections have been postponed as well. The

Chapter Twenty-nine – Northern Ireland

Unionist party, central to any settlement, is severely divided between those who are broadly sympathetic to the Good Friday agreement and those who reject it.

Leaving aside the internal problems of the Unionist party, and taking a wider view of the various competing parties, it now seems inevitable that if the electoral process was to be resumed then most uncompromising candidates from all sides would be the ones most likely to get elected.

That prospect alone may deter the government from holding fresh elections.

Without such elections there can be no new assembly. Without an Assembly there can be no Executive.

In which case Northern Ireland will continue to be governed like a colony by Order in Council from the Committee Corridor of the House of Commons. This is compounded by the fact that Northern Ireland has no local government system bearing any comparison with what we have in England.

One and a half million of our fellow United Kingdom citizens are left with their problems but neither the power nor the concomitant challenge nor the institutions even to do anything about them.

I conclude with this paradox. Despite all that I have said, Northern Ireland remains one of the most beautiful places I have ever visited and the vast majority of its citizens are warm, charming, amusing, generous and hospitable. And they *are* our fellow citizens.

The one thing we cannot do about Northern Ireland is to pretend that it does not exist or just hope that it will go away.

Chapter 30

Secretaries

I thank my lucky stars

Apart from Irene Freeth, who has an honourable mention elsewhere, the two secretaries who have made my varied and interesting career possible, manageable, effective and indeed enjoyable are Mavis Ferguson [1] and Paula Barnes. Mavis has worked for me for over 30 years, straddling the law and politics, and is still my part-time consultant.

Paula worked alongside Mavis when I was in the European Parliment doing my E.P. work and returned to be my front line secretary in August 2000 when Mavis worthily preferred a part-time commitment 3 years ago.

Their true job title has always escaped description by me. "Secretary" is inadequate, "Personal Assistant" (or "PA"), an Americanism, does not describe the job either. The reality is that, in my natural absences in Westminster, they have actually been something approaching "Assistant Member of Parliament for Solihull". No such job exists under our constitution. But that's really what they have done. I thank them and, I dare say, many others will want to thank them too.

---

1. Her husband G.B. "Gibby" Ferguson fought through World War 2 with great distinction with the Scots Guards.

Chapter 31

My Father

The unassuming influence of the flawed God

I have been casting around in my mind for a literary or dramatic allusion that might suit my purpose as of a part in a play or a character in a story who does not appear very often or have many lines but who has a significant influence on the whole thread of the tale, whilst almost not wishing to.

When I was born, a war baby, my father, then reduced by illness to seven stone in weight, was unable to lift me out of my cot. His affliction was ankylosing spondylitis which my Oxford Dictionary describes as 'a form of spinal arthritis, chiefly affecting young males …'. In my story the 'young male' was my father. This intelligent, good-looking, witty, exuberant (it got him into trouble too) and well-coordinated man, he had been a good games player, was gradually being crippled in front of my mother who was in despair. It stooped him forwards from the neck and from lower than the neck and stiffened his rib cage and limited his movement, in particular his ability to turn sideways. He must have also been in pain.

My mother's parents and a childless aunt of my mother spared nothing on consultations with the finest specialists. Some years later my father was to tell me that he knew Harley Street quite well because he had been up and down both sides of it. No relief came. He tried all manner of unorthodox medicine too.

Then suddenly the disease stopped. It made no further dreadful progress. It just stopped. He did not straighten up again or lose his stiffness. It left him as he was. He began to put on weight and strength. From the wretched seven stone which he was when I was born, he gradually went up to thirteen stone, quite 'chunky' for a man no taller than me.

Then, remarkably at the age of forty when most active men would normally be thinking of giving it up, he announced that he was going to start playing cricket again. And he did. He played until he was fifty. Then he started umpiring.

He was quite a useful batsman. His ability to drive the ball was limited but, like quite a lot of short men, he could cut and hook and pull fiercely and he had an elegant leg glance or glide. He was limited to an underarm throw but almost invariably fielded in the slips where he could get away with that limitation. He used to incur some fearful bruises from opening the batting against fast bowling and showed me them with pride.

On one occasion, keeping wicket, he broke a finger so badly that the doctor told him it could either be set rigid for the rest of his life or it could be amputated. He told me about this and I pleaded with him to keep his finger.

On another occasion I saw him helped from the field after being hit on the head by a bouncer. He went for the hook shot and was, classically correctly, attempting to hit the ball 'off his eyebrows', as they say. The only difficulty is that if you miss the ball it is still heading for your eyebrows and you have absolutely no time for evasion. That is exactly what happened. His face was quite a mess and he was bleeding quite heavily as he was led into the pavilion for some first aid.

My brother and I who had seen this and were quite concerned decided, nonetheless, that it was a matter for adults and that we would simply remain watching the cricket.

After about fifteen minutes, or twenty minutes at the most, a wicket fell, the batsman who was out was walking off the field when father emerged from the pavilion with his head quite heavily bandaged, walked out to the crease and, resuming his innings, went on batting.

Sometimes I think that having defied the disease he was determined to defy everything else. But tales of his boyhood would suggest that he was always a physical risk taker and always defiant.

He was well liked and had many friends but I suspect many of them would occasionally have taken leave to doubt his judgement. They would not have doubted his courage.

He was a good father, but I suspect, sometimes an exasperating husband but we all loved him.

His working career was relatively successful, if not exceptionally highly paid and he spent the last twelve or thirteen years until he retired at the age of sixty four as a main board director of a plc with responsibility for sales. The product being heavy electrical engineering equipment, generators for power stations or ships, that sort of thing.

At his retirement party, a dinner which I attended, he made a short speech which was a delicious blend of his mischief, his wisdom and his tendency to self mockery. In this speech he praised the virtues of what he called 'Management by Guesswork'. He said that decision-making in industry was too slow and that there were many times when it was better to make an informed guess and get on with it. He claimed Napoleon in aid of this proposition saying that Napoleon could make decisions so fast that

Chapter Thirty-one – My Father

it hardly mattered if they were wrong because the enemy was always taken by surprise. Of course he could have referred to 'intuition based on experience' but 'guesswork' was more brazen. So he preferred guesswork. His audience enjoyed the speech and were entertained by it. None of them knew whether he was being entirely serious and that, I think, is why he enjoyed it too.

He could write beautifully. Mainly he wrote about cricket. It was humourous and human. His chosen pen name was 'Wormcast', in itself an original, if slightly excessive, piece of self-deprecation.

After our mother's death, father died before her, my brother and I were going through some of father's belongings and Michael kindly agreed that I could have the limited number of his published articles which we managed to find.

I read my way through them including the one in which he himself writes that it is to be his last, his swan-song. Apologising for the fact that the publisher will have to find someone else in future he adds: "... I have a relative who says he is prepared to bash out an article if you are ever stuck. I don't know if he can write, but he can certainly talk".

He meant me.

He had a huge range of interests especially in the accounts of heroic mountaineering expeditions: Annapurna, K2, Kanchenjunga, Nanga Parbat and, of course, Everest. On reading father's copy of the book called "K2 The Savage Mountain" by Charles Houston and Robert Bates, I found in it a postcard addressed to my father calling itself "COMMEMORATIVE COVER FROM BASE CAMP". It is post marked "Annapurna south face expedition BASE CAMP." It carries the signatures of ten of the climbers headed by that of Chris Bonnington. It makes clear that the Annapurna south face expedition of 1970 is about to begin its ascent. It is safe to assume that the climbing team had arranged the dispatch of these postcards with pre-fixed labels and an awesome photograph of the south face on the other side as an appreciation to those who had subscribed in support of the expedition. Clearly father had been a subscriber. This, I am sure, was the true world of his imagination. He was not merely fascinated by these awesome mountain ventures, he would actually have liked to have been on them, as one of the climbers.

This unusual, stoic man seldom showed me any affection unless I was in real distress such as after I had crashed his car at the age of nineteen and been brought home by the police. Mercifully no-one had been hurt by my driving off the road. He merely responded to my wretchedness. He must have felt that no rebuke was necessary.

Please Stay To The Adjournment

This chapter has not been an attempt at a mini-biography of Wilfred 'Bill' Taylor. It is, at most, an insight.

Nor is this collection of episodes, as a whole, anymore than an incidental autobiography of me.

I am content for father and I to bring down the curtain together.

We were watching the news on television. There was a dreadful, vast riot somewhere in the Third World. Even on an early television set it was clear that the numbers were enormous and filled the screen, shouting, fighting, protesting.

"Do you know John," he said to me, "that probably not one of them could bowl a decent off-break?"

Goodnight, Dad. And, by the way thanks again.

INDEX

A.

ADAMSON, CAMPBELL ...50
ALLSOP, MARTIN ...33, 34, 35
ALLSOP & CO ...34
AMPHLETT, DON ...19
ARBUTHNOT, JAMES ...111, 113, 117

B.

BARNES, PAULA ...122
BARRETT, BRENDA ...47
BATES, ROBERT ...125
BEAUMONT-DARK, SIR ANTHONY ...52, 55, 78, *II*
BELL, MARTIN ...106
BENN, TONY ...109
BERCOW, JOHN ...114, 115
BERGHELLI, CORRADO ...30
BERRY, MR AND MRS ...2
BERRY, MARY ...2
BETJEMAN, JOHN ...20
BETTS, CLIVE ...114
BEVAN, DAVID GILROY ...52, 79, *II*
BLOW, PAULINE ...107
BONINGTON, SIR CHRIS ...125
BOOTHROYD, BETTY ...109
BOSWELL, TIM ...114, 115
BRANDON-BRAVO, MARTIN ...81
BRANDT, WILLI ...67
BRONOWSKI, PROFESSOR ...12
BROOKE, PETER ...116
BRUNEL, ISAMBARD KINGDOM ...22

C.

CAHOON, KEN ...2
CALLAGHAN, JIM ...59, 61
CAREY, LIONEL ...19
CARR, DONALD ...27
CARSON ...119

CARSON, JOE ...17
CATHERWOOD, SIR FRED ...6
CEZANNE ...94
CHAPMAN, DENYS ...43
CHARLIE, BONNIE PRINCE ...101
CHIRAC, JACQUES ...67
CHRIST, JESUS ...57, 58
CHURCHILL, WINSTON S ...118
CLARKE, KENNETH ...79, 80, 82, 110, 111
CLOUGH, GORDON ...78
COLEMAN, REVEREND ...7
COLLETT, TONY ...25
COLLINS, MICHAEL ...120
COLLODI, HELEN ...89
COOKES, SIR THOMAS ...14
COOMBES, ALDERMAN LES ...41, 43
CRAIG ...119
CRENSHAW, BEN ...27

D.

DANIEL ...57
DAY, ROBIN ...78
DARWIN, BERNARD ...24
DERRINGTON, PETER ...7
DISRAELI, BENJAMIN ...75
DORRELL, STEPHEN ...86, 110

E.

EDINBURGH, DUKE OF ...*V*
EDMISTER, JIM ...2
ELIJAH ...57
ELIZABETH, H.M. QUEEN ...*X*
ELLIS, MIKE ...61

F.

FELLOWES, ROBERT ...*VIII*

G.

GAREL-JONES, TRISTAN ...x
GARDNER, TRIXIE ...61
GEORGE I, KING ...83
GEORGE II, KING ...83
GIBBON, DON ...18
GILBERT, LORD (JOHN) ...50
GILKS, PAUL ...36
GILMAN, CONGRESSMAN BEN ...*VI*
GLADSTONE, WILLIAM ...118, 119
GOEBBELS, DR. ...87
GOODLAD, ALASTAIR ...*VII*
GORMLEY, JOE ...50
GRAY, DENIS ...37, 38
GRAY, GILBERT ...92
GREEN, DAMIEN ...114, 115
GREGSON, PETER ...97
GRICE, JOHN ...19, 32
GRIEVE, PERCY ...73
GRIFFIN, SIR FRANCIS ...44, 45, 52
GRIFFITHS, COUNCILLOR BOB ...49
GRIFFITHS, ALDERMAN GEORGE ...47, 48, 49
GRIFFITHS, SIR EDEN ...87

H.

HADLEY, PAUL ...96, 100
HAGUE, WILLIAM ...110, 111, 117, *IX*
HAMMOND, PHILIP ...114, 115
HAPSBURG, OTTO VAN ...66
HARDMAN, SIR FRED ...59
HARRIS, BILL ...53
HAMILTON, NEIL ...106
HANNIBAL ...17
HAYCOCK, MICHAEL ...40
HEATH, EDWARD ...44, 50, 67, *II*
HEATHCOTE, AMORY ...86
HEDLEY, JOHN (JUNGLE JIM) ...19
HENDER, DERRYCK ...55, 56
HESELTINE, MICHAEL ...88, 97
HILL, REVEREND ...7
HINCHLIFFE, ALICE ...20
HINCHLIFFE, PETER ...20
HOBSON, REG ...76

HOLBROOK, JONATHAN ...94
HOPE, ALAN ...53
HOUSTON, CHARLES ...125
HOWARD, MICHAEL ...92, 110, 111
HOWE, MRS ...40
HUCKFIELD, LES ...62
HUMBERSTONE, VINCENT ...40
HURD, DOUGLAS ...88

I.

ISAIAH ...57

J.

JARUZELSKI, GENERAL ...vii
JOLLIE, IAIN ...38
JONES, JACK ...68

K.

KARLE, STEPHEN ...36
KENNEDY, PRESIDENT ...55
KING, MALCOLM ...37
KING, ROGER ...78
KOLBUSZOWSKI, PROFESSOR ...20

L.

LANG, IAN ...97, 98
LANGLEY, WALTER ...40, 41
LANSLEY, NIGEL ...61
LAWSON, NIGEL ...18
LEPINE, MONSIEUR ...18
LEWIS, DON ...46
LIGHTBOWN, SIR DAVID ...ix, 82, *VII*
LILLEY, PETER ...110, 111
LINDLEY, P.C ...1
LING, JOHN DE COURCY ...60, 61
LINDSAY, SIR MARTIN ...73
LIVINGSTONE, KEN ...80, 116
LONGHURST, HENRY ...24
LUCAS ...22
LYON, CLARK & CO ...28, 29, 30, 39

Index

M.

MACDONALD, JOYCE ...49
MACKAY, ANDREW ...74, 91
MAIGRET ...22
MAINWARING, CAPTAIN ...1
MAJOR, JOHN ...88, 89, 90, 106, 110, 111, 120, *IX*
MANDELSON, PETER ...97
MANTHORPE, JOHN ...93
MARGARET, PRINCESS ...42
MARY, QUEEN ...14
MAYHEW, LORD (PATRICK) ...90
MILES, RON ...25
MITCHELL, PETER ...73
MITTERAND, PRESIDENT ...ix
MOLIERE ...18
MONET ...93, 94
MONTGOMERY, FIELD MARSHAL SIR BERNARD ...19
MOSES ...57
MUSSOLINI, BENITO ...67

N.

NAPOLEON ...18
NATTRASS, MIKE ...107
NOCK, O.S ...21

O.

O'SULLIVAN, TERRY ...62

P.

PARKINSON, CECIL ...107
PARR, DAWN ...100
PEACOCK, REVEREND ...7, 8
PERREY, PETER ...28, 34, 36
PFLIMLIN, PIERRE ...66, 67
PHILLIPS, BRIAN ...89
PITTS, JOHN ...93
PLANT, STANLEY ...60
PLUMB, SIR HENRY ...33
POLLARD, GEOFFREY ...7
POLYZOIDES, JOHN ...72, 103

POPE, THE ...*IV*
POWELL, ENOCH ...118
PREEDY, LUING ...47, 48, 49

R.

"RANJI" ...70
REDFERN, SIR HERBERT ...59, 60
REDMAN, JOHN ...20
REDWOOD, JOHN ...110, 111
REYNOLD, & CO ...22, 28, 29, 32, 33, 34, 35
RICHARDS, COUNCILLOR GILBERT ...52
RICHARDSON, D.N ...9
RICHARDSON, P.E (PETER) ...9
ROLAND, EVANS AND TAYLOR ...35
ROOT, PETER ...22, 28, 29, 33, 34, 37
ROSSI, SIR HUGH ...75
ROUTH, R.G ...14
ROTH, ANDREW ...79
ROWLAND, "TINY" ...97
ROWLEY, JOE ...50

S.

SACKVILLE, TOM ...86
SARAZEN, GENE ...24
SAUNDERS, PAUL ...36
SCARGILL, ARTHUR ...50, 68
SCOTT-HOPKINS, JIM ...64, 65
SEAGROTT, EDGAR ...38
SISLEY ...94
SLESSER, SUE ...59
SMITH, COUNCILLOR ...52
SMITH, F.E ...90
SMITH, HERMAN ...48, 49
SMITH, JOHN ...79
SPELMAN, CAROLINE ...116
SPINELLI, ALTIERO ...66
STOBART, EDWARD (EDDIE) ...96
STOCKDALE, DR CHRIS ...102, 103
SUTHERLAND, PETER ...80

T.

TAYLOR, ALLSOP & CO ...34, 123, 124, 125, 126

Please Stay To The Adjournment

TAYLOR, ANNE ...39
TAYLOR, ERIC ...39
TAYLOR, GEORGE ...31
TAYLOR, JOHN (NAMESAKE) ...63
TAYLOR, GRANDAD AND GRANNY ...5, 10
TAYLOR, JOHN & CO ...23, 34, 35
TAYLOR, MICHAEL ...3, 125
TAYLOR, PETER ...35
TAYLOR, WILFRED ...35
TAYLORS ...35
TEBBIT, NORMAN ...78
THATCHER, MARGARET ...vii, viii, 51, 60,
    61, 64, 65, 74, 78, 79, 87, 92, *IV*
THORNHAM, PETER ...94
TINDERMANS, LEE ...67
TOTO ...18
TROTMAN, MR ...8
TUPPEN, TED ...37
TYACK, MRS SARAH ...93

V.

VALERA, EAMON DE ...120
VAZ, KEITH ...89
VICTORIA, QUEEN ...103

W.

WADDINGTON, DAVID ...83
WALKER, PETER ...44, 73, 79, 87
WALPOLE ...83
WALTER, D.J ...14, 15
WARDLE, CHARLES ...74
WARNER, SIR FRED ...60
WARREN-WIND, HERBERT ...24
WILSON, HAROLD ...51
WILSON, LEONARD ...37
WILSON, RAE ...32
WODEHOUSE, P.G ...24
WOOD, ALFIE ...1

XYZ.

YOUNG, BRENDA ...107, 112
YOUNG, JIMMY ...78
YOUNG, LORD (DAVID) ...80, 82